ADVANCE PRAISE FOR
# GED Stories

"With passion and insight, Joanne Kilgour Dowdy presents the compelling stories of courage and determination as told by Black women who took the 'GED journey.' Dowdy allows the voices of the women to predominate and carry this documentation and analysis of marginalization and hope. She demonstrates through these cases the ways that racism, gender bias, and classism continue to shape the opportunities of Black women in the United States today. In the process, she gives us a glimpse of the underside of the promise of the GED program. Without significant structural change to society, too many Black women, despite having attained this degree, will continue to be forced to accept non-mainstream forms of employment just '...to keep body and soul together.'"

*Victoria Purcell-Gates, Michigan State University*

"Through the voices of four Black women, Joanne Dowdy brings us close and personal to those aspects in GED programs that liberate and facilitate Black women in their struggle between educational attainment and the quality of life choices. She also brings to the forefront the inadequacy Black women experience when these programs do not sharpen their ability to examine and act on issues of power, oppression, dominance, race, class, and gender within social structures and economic arrangements. The need for alternative teaching methods in GED programs is strong and well documented. Dr. Dowdy, a compassionate, creative scholar, expertly shows how the use of the liberating aspects of a culture creates opportunities for discovery and inquiry into one's self, community and institutions. This study clarifies the concept that the literacies of a person or a people transcend reading and writing and are the very essence of what it means to be liberated. This book will help all of us who are working in adult literacy and GED programs to conceptualize the degree to which skills can be used in liberating ways so that participants can better understand and transform themselves and their world."

*Liz Peavy, Executive Director, Septima Clark Center for Urban Literacy*

# GED Stories

# Studies in the Postmodern Theory of Education

Joe L. Kincheloe and Shirley R. Steinberg
*General Editors*

Vol. 228

PETER LANG
New York • Washington, D.C./Baltimore • Bern
Frankfurt am Main • Berlin • Brussels • Vienna • Oxford

Joanne Kilgour Dowdy

# GED Stories

## Black Women & Their Struggle for Social Equity

PETER LANG
New York • Washington, D.C./Baltimore • Bern
Frankfurt am Main • Berlin • Brussels • Vienna • Oxford

**Library of Congress Cataloging-in-Publication Data**

Dowdy, Joanne Kilgour.
GED stories: Black women and their struggle for social equity / Joanne Kilgour Dowdy.
p. cm. — (Counterpoints: studies in the postmodern theory of education; v. 228)
Includes bibliographical references and index.
1. African American women—Education—Case studies. 2. Adult education—
United States—Case studies. 3. General educational development tests—Case studies.
4. Functional literacy—United States—Case studies. 5. Educational equalization—
United States—Case studies. I. Title. II. Counterpoints (New York, N.Y.); v. 228.
LC2780.8 .D69    373.1829'96—dc21    2002070489
ISBN 0-8204-6215-2
ISSN 1058-1634

**Die Deutsche Bibliothek-CIP-Einheitsaufnahme**

Dowdy, Joanne Kilgour:
GED stories: black women and their struggle for social equity / Joanne Kilgour Dowdy.
–New York; Washington, D.C./Baltimore; Bern;
Frankfurt am Main; Berlin; Brussels; Vienna; Oxford: Lang.
(Counterpoints; Vol. 228)
ISBN 0-8204-6215-2

Permission was granted to reprint from the *Journal of Literacy Research*
V 33, I, pp. 71–98
Cover photo by Matthew Weinstein
Cover design by Joni Holst

© 2003 Peter Lang Publishing, Inc., New York
275 Seventh Avenue, 28th Floor, New York, NY 10001
www.peterlangusa.com

All rights reserved.
Reprint or reproduction, even partially, in all forms such as microfilm,
xerography, microfiche, microcard, and offset strictly prohibited.

*For*

*Reverend Swami Tathagatananda*

# Contents

Acknowledgments  ix

ONE
Background of the Study  1

TWO
Carmen Montana  16

THREE
Carolee Carpenter  27

FOUR
Maria Walters  34

FIVE
Evelyn Anderson  42

SIX
Cross-Case Analysis  48

APPENDIX
Interviews  67

References  95

Index  99

# Acknowledgments

I sincerely appreciate the support and technical assistance that I received over the years that this book was being created from: Dr. James Cunningham, Dr. Martha Abbott-shim, Dr. Lisa Delpit, Dr. Joanne R. Nurss, and Dr. Nancy Padak. There are many other people who are too numerous to list here who must also be thanked. I hope that they know that I appreciate everything that they did in word and deed to encourage me in this journey.

It is also important that I thank the courageous graduate students who took on the initial project of finding and interviewing the GED graduates who are mentioned in Chapter Two. Without Miranda Sidor, Dr. Yvette Walters, Raquel Pottinger-Bird, and Dr. Irene Lawson, I might still be wondering if I could complete the interviews with these GED graduates in this century.

Finally, and most important, Lori Wolnik made this manuscript readable. A world of thanks to her for her patience.

ONE

# Background of the Study

I am a Black woman from Trinidad, an island in the Caribbean. I came to the United States twenty-one years ago as a college student. As I moved from Boston, to New York, to North Carolina, and then to Georgia, I realized that my status as Black woman was always being assigned to me through the stereotypes that White people and non-White Americans presented in their interactions with me. Why did my color always signify a lower socioeconomic status? Why was my accent a signifier of a lower educational level than I had attained at graduate school? These questions haunted me as I began to look around at the low-paying jobs that most Black women held in North Carolina and Georgia. The implications of the answers to the questions led me to ask what a GED (General Education Diploma) "really" meant if the chances of being promoted in a White establishment were less than slim and to what extent the attainment of that "high school" level of literacy impacted the way in which a Black woman made a living for herself and her family.

The idea for this study came to me after completing the case study of Carmen Montana and her social network. In that study, I looked at the way that the social network, her closest family and friends, supported Montana in her quest for the GED (see pp. 80–95). My findings showed that the social network played a significant role in Montana's journey before, during, and after she attained the certificate. Once those findings were reported, I found myself wondering about the experience of other Black women who had achieved the high school equivalency certificate. With the help of three graduate students and teachers from several literacy training sites, I contacted nine women who were willing to speak with us about their experiences in the GED journey. Why did these women drop out of high school? How long did it take them to decide to return to formal schooling? What impact, if any, did the increase in their literacy training have on their lives and on their family and friends? These questions represented the beginning of the present collection of GED stories.

## *The General Educational Diploma*

The General Education Diploma (GED) Tests are promoted as a key to opportunities, advancement, further education, and financial rewards. The GED is composed of five tests that include writing skills, social studies, interpreting literature and the arts, science, and mathematics. The tests are designed to measure the general skills and knowledge usually acquired in a four-year high school program of study. The point of the tests is to look at the student's ability to evaluate, analyze, and then draw conclusions, combined with the capacity to understand and apply information and concepts *(GED 2000 Statistical Report: Who Took the GED?,* 2002).

Between 1990 and 2000, over three-quarter of a million people took the GED battery of tests. Of those, 500,000 achieved the high school equivalency diploma. Statistics on the high school diplomas awarded in the United States claim that one of seven of these diplomas is based on the successful completion of the battery of tests provided by the GED. Those who take the GED represent a range of backgrounds of experiences: recent high school students, some people who have been out of school for a long time, and others who may be as old as eighty and still pursuing educational training.

In the year 2000, only 1.5% of the adults who did not graduate from high school attempted the GED tests. Of those, just 1% earned the high school equivalency credential *(GED 2000 Statistical Report: Who Took the GED?,* 2002). It is also reported that the number of adults who plan to go on to higher education programs after attaining their diploma has increased 21.4% since 1943. This represents the persistence of GED graduates in the face of the fact that the new passing rate for the GED tests is set at a standard that exceeds the performance of at least 33% of high school seniors. Once the passing rate was increased in North Carolina and Georgia, the number of students who achieved the diploma dropped to 64.8% from its 1996 level of 70.4%.

In Georgia, it is reported that every year 19,000 people graduate with the GED credential. According to Kathy Lee, director of the assessment, evaluation, and GED administration, the GED "is not an easy thing to do . . . it takes a certain kind of person to see it through." Advocates of the GED believe that employers view the GED graduate as someone who will persist in efforts to succeed. Since it is possible to redo separate tests in the exam, many of the students who make up the 72% pass rate each year are repeat examinees, which is further proof of their persistence.

The review of the statistics shows that having the GED degree opened doors to further education, in colleges and other settings, and promotions on the job (Baldwin, 1995) and that these graduates earn wages at 8% higher levels per year than high school dropouts.

Further, GED graduates are significantly more likely than dropouts to be in the labor force and be employed full-time and they are employed at a 5% higher pay rate than dropouts (Boesel, 1998). They are also more frequently in line to receive additional training after earning their credential (Murnane, Willett, and Boudett, 1994), and to expect that their wages will grow at a faster rate than dropouts (Murnane, Willett, and Boudett, cited in Brewer, 1993).

Research on the literacy skills attained by GED graduates, compared to high school graduates, shows that people who pass the GED tests demonstrate literacy skills reflecting a level of literacy widely viewed as necessary for social and economic advancement and for exercising the rights and responsibilities of citizenship (Baldwin, Kirsch, Rock, and Yamamoto, 1995). However, the GED process, from the first class to the receipt of the diploma, represents a high school level of cognitive skills, and does not assure that graduates have attained the quality of work habits, perseverance, and organizational socialization that traditional high school students are able to attain at the end of their 861 hours more of core curriculum subject study (Boesel, 1998).

In a report on the reasons that many African Americans do not attend adult literacy programs and the motivations for those that do, Denny (1996) observed that among those who do, "a burning desire within the individual" was usually set ablaze due to an event like "an inability to complete a task, a change in family situation, or observance of how destructive low literacy can be" (p. 16). Another reason cited for the involvement in the adult literacy class is the fact that adult learners want to do things with the same level of comfort that they see literate people doing. Adult learners are also found to be motivated by the possibilities they project for their future, the choices that they perceive in their lives, and their belief in the potential for change in their circumstances (Luttrell, 1997).

In addition, adult literacy students find that their need to be of use to their children, church members, and community (Dowdy, 2001) plays a significant role in their determination to complete literacy courses. Jacqueline Peck (1993) also found that GED students looked to their family, friends, and peers for support in their journey as literacy students. The support system that the GED student manages to establish before, during, and after the GED journey is a significant part of the experience of completing the high school-level training. This kind of social engagement brings the adult learner into a community of like minds, and the experience of group support makes the involvement in literacy training an attractive alternative to the kinds of despair and discouragement that Sloan, Jason, and Addlesperger (1996) cited in their report.

### *Challenges to Participation in Adult Literacy Programs*

The difficulty of the circumstances in which candidates operate is a tremendous challenge to the resolve to improve their circumstances. Philipsen (1993) captured the sense of being overwhelmed by circumstances in the response of one of the participants in her study. The woman opined:

> It came like a shock to me. All of a sudden I found myself with a child, working in a fast-food restaurant. That's why I was saying that education is important because I know I could be doing something better.... I didn't know how hard it would be without finishing school. Now if I could go back to school I would. (p. 421)

Even when adults choose to participate in adult literacy programs, they are confronted with the paucity of programs that exist. Irwin S. Kirsh of Education Testing Service confirms the fact that "disparities in opportunity to learn, suitable academic counseling, and the quality of teaching and instructional resources" affect the literacy proficiencies and academic skills of White, Hispanic and African-American adult students (cited in Merkowitz and Wilcox, 1996, p. 3).

In the same study it was found that White GED examinees displayed higher literacy skills than Hispanic or African-American examinees, with the latter performing at the lowest level in the exam. Kirsch suggests that these findings indicate a need for ways to improve pre- and post-testing, curriculum, instruction, and counseling for adult learners from diverse ethnic, racial, and cultural backgrounds.

Peck's study of GED students showed the ways in which the social network operated to support or hinder GED students on the journey to their certificates. Much like the results from Fingeret's (1983) study of low literates, it is clear that "network patterns" shift once a student enrolls in a class to increase his or her literacy skills. The student's strong commitment to learn in the face of the challenge of a new or crumbling network system can create a source of tremendous discomfort among group members. Because of this change in the social network pattern and the kinds of support activities that the group traditionally provided for itself, it is clear that the decision of the literacy student to venture out in the world and to be exposed to experiences otherwise unavailable to the rest of the network is a considerable challenge to the status quo of the group (Rockhill, 1990).

## *Black Women in the Workforce*

It is a fact that throughout the course of this country's history most Blacks have lived near or below the poverty line (Farley, 1997). This exacerbated situation is inflamed by the fact that other factors in the environments of Black women do not help the situation. For example, a study by Critzer (1998) found that their income did not improve significantly as a result of the wealth of a state, the number of women legislators, party competition, or the number of Black state legislators. His study emphasized that any further reduction in state support for affirmative action would represent a continued decrease in income parity for minorities and women. The fact that economic restructuring has discouraged urban industrial development and consequently provided fewer manufacturing jobs for Blacks (Wilson, 1980) further demonstrates the lack of opportunities for Black women with low skills.

According to Farley (1997), the odds of minorities being unemployed from 1980 to 1990 relative to Whites increased significantly compared to previous years. On the other hand, the positive impact of the unionization of jobs in manufacturing industries (Grant and Parcel, 1990; Maume, 1985) shows some of the few openings for Black female mobility in an otherwise bleak employment picture. Until 1995, Black women were still earning only 90% of the median incomes of White women (Farley, 1997). Overall, it seems that, the grim picture for Black women's employment constricts the viability of the pursuit of academic credentials.

Even if Black women could get their foot in the door of a business, a federal commission on the status of women and minorities in the largest private industries reported that the leaders of these businesses held to an unspoken law that kept this group of citizens out of the highest ranking jobs in the country (U.S. Federal Glass Ceiling Commission, 1995). Men and women who did not fit the corporate image of White men faced a glass ceiling constructed to keep them out of the highest levels of decision making.

We need to consider, therefore (a) the fact that there is a need for the transformation of Black women's labor, presently tied to the structure of the state and economy as well as to features of the racial/gender division of labor (Critzer, 1998; Epstein, 1973), and (b) the reality of Black women being mostly employed in federal jobs, at lower wages than Whites, if not totally unemployed (Beggs, 1995), to understand the context in which Black women might seek higher educational qualifications.

## *The Study*

From 1999 to 2000 I spent time with my graduate students interviewing nine Black women graduates of the GED program. It was a long process to contact these graduates and then to convince them to talk with us. Although the GED is touted as a "good" thing in our society (Baldwin, 1995), some graduates of this high school equivalency test are very reluctant to declare that they have this academic credential. They are even more reluctant to talk about their journey to make the decision to study and then sit for the qualifying examination.

It would be easy for me to say that once my research team, consisting of five graduate students from various doctoral programs in education at the university where I taught, contacted these women and began their series of interviews, things went well for us. This was not necessarily the case. In a sense, once the interviews were completed we felt that we had scored a major victory. Then the analysis of the transcripts began and I, for one, began a journey of resistance to the information in the interviews. I had set up the research project to capture the voices of Black women who had a success story to share. It was also my intent to document the journey of these women because there is not much published material that tells the story of Black women who have achieved the GED.

Many high school students believe that they can leave school with an eighth-grade level of literacy and still be successful at attaining the GED. These young people do not realize that they must command the literacy level of a twelfth-grade student if they are going to succeed in the high school equivalency test (Merkowitz and Wilcox, 1996). Also, Black women have long believed that they will be hired faster and be promoted more quickly if they are able to present a GED certificate to their employers. The research by Brewer (1993), however, shows that White women are more likely to be promoted across the board, regardless of the level of their experience, compared with Black women. Consequently, I have a few problems getting excited about the so-called ability of the GED to ensure that Black adults begin an upward climb to financial stability and academic success (Baldwin, 1995).

## The Women in the Study

We looked at nine Black women in the initial study. The women's ages varied from nineteen to forty-two years old. The average age of the women when they dropped out of school was sixteen years and the average age of the women in the group was thirty-four years old. It seems that the women began their GED journey during the "Age of 30 Transition" period (Levinson and Levinson, cited in Merriam and Caffarella, 1999). All but one of the women in the group we interviewed had gotten married at some point before we had met them. Long before the women began the GED journey they already had at least one child. The nine women in the study had about four children each among them.

In this transition period of people in their thirties, women and men are likely to question their current life status, and sometimes make drastic life changes in various aspects of their lives. These women described several reasons for making their decision to return to the traditional classroom for literacy training. The rationales included a feeling of discontent with their educational level and/or their job; lack of communication skills; a poor self-image as non-achieving adults; limited socioeconomic skills; inadequate parenting skills; a strong sense of dependency; and, finally, a desire for higher educational skills.

The four women who are described in the following chapters, Carmen, C.C., Maria, and Evelyn, each have between one and six children, are married, and three of them were employed at the time of the interviews. Three of the women were considering returning to college in order to continue their education. One of the women had published two books and had already achieved degrees in teacher education and business.

## *The Interview Protocol*

When we began our interviews with the nine Black women in our study, we had three broad questions in mind (Seidman, 1991). They were: (1) How she came to her GED certificate. The goal was to find out as much as possible about her life leading up to her present position or to her status as a GED graduate; (2) Find out as much as possible about the details of her GED graduate status. For example, what is her work? What is it like for her to do what she does now that she is a graduate? (3) What does her experience as a GED graduate mean to her? In other words, now that she has talked about how she came to her GED classes, and what it is like for her to be a graduate, what does it mean to her?

Each woman was asked these three questions, one question on each day that she met with an interviewer, at sessions that lasted from forty to sixty minutes each.

The initial prompt, how she came to her GED certificate, was followed up by questions like "What was happening in your life?" "What was the main reason that you stopped going to school when you were younger?" "At what age did you realize that you can't help anybody until you help yourself?" Or, "How did your family respond when you told them you wanted to go back to get your GED at age forty?"

Our aim was to find out as much as possible about the woman's background before she made the decision to begin the GED program. Our probes were meant to gather information about the kind of life that the woman was involved in when she realized that she was not content with her educational status and needed to add some academic training to her list of skills. The interview data revealed interesting life stories that told a good deal about the kind of dissatisfaction that occurred at different points in each woman's life.

The question that we asked when we met on the second interview—ask the participant to tell us as much as possible about the details of her GED graduate status—"What is your work? What is it like for you to do what you do now that you are a graduate?" We followed up with prompts like: "Do you think you could have done what you're doing now without your GED?" "So, what is it like for you in your personal life . . . now that you're a GED graduate?" "How did the GED journey affect your children?" "Are you doing different things now than you planned to do when you got the certificate?"

In this second interview, we were concerned with capturing the picture of the GED journey from beginning to end. We wanted to know what it was like to be in the particular GED program that each woman attended over the course of her GED studies. Our intention was to see the GED journey through the eyes of the student, the Black woman with children, who made the decision to turn her life around and face the challenges that making that commitment represented. We found that the women talked about the ways in which their family, children, and friends figured in the experience that led to their completion of the GED course. People told us of many reasons for the motivation to be successful in the GED program.

In the final interview with the women, we asked about their interpretation of the GED experience from the beginning to the day on which we spoke to each of them. Our prompt—"Now that you have talked about how you came to your GED classes and what it is like for you to be a graduate, what does it mean to you?"—was designed to solicit a reflective response to the experience of making the decision to return to school. We wanted to know how each woman felt about completing the GED course and then going on to make a different life from what they were experiencing at the beginning of the journey.

The women, in general, talked about their pride in themselves for completing one task that they set out to do. They also shared their feelings about the changes that took place in their family, especially their children, once they completed the GED course and secured a certificate. Many of the women, mostly the mothers, talked about the importance of setting a good example for their children. They did not want them to be tempted to drop out of school and be exposed to the difficult experiences of working for a minimum wage. Nor did they want them to be embarrassed about their occupation when they had to fill out forms for employment.

## *Method*

We followed Lincoln and Guba's (1985) recommendations for data analysis, including triangulation, prolonged engagement, peer debriefing, member checks, and thick description. The study developed inductively with categories and questions emerging from the data provided by the nine women, and then these were refined into focused questions that were used to identify answers that were provided in the transcripts of the women's interviews.

After reading the transcripts of the audiotaped interviews, each member of the research team did preliminary coding based on emerging themes. Using constant comparison (Strauss & Corbin, 1990), each of us compared and discussed our findings and coordinated initial codes. The entire team then reanalyzed data to confirm categories, make final changes, and reach consensus on the titles that would be used to represent the data themes. During the second review of the transcripts, we paid close attention to the descriptions of "character" that each participant provided.

## Black Women and Society

My response to these stories could be constructed as a general inability to deal with reality as it exists in many public schools. The reality for many Black children and others of non-White heritage is that they find the schools as they are today alienating places full of White middle-class values (Delpit, 1995). More important, my discomfort with the facts of these women's lives could be located in that place that is always alive with the awareness that I am a woman of color, a Black woman, who has to face the challenges of living in a society that is greatly influenced by its adherence to class and color distinctions (Davis, 1983). My unease around the stories that these women shared with me comes most certainly from my lived experience (Dowdy, 1999). I know why the "caged bird sings," as poet Paul Laurence Dunbar (Braxton, 1993) told us in his famous poem.

To be Black and female in this country is to bear the burden of racism, sexism, and classism (Lerner, 1972). It means that you have to challenge the societal expectations that say that you are incapable of rising to a level of excellence that other members of society can achieve (Harley and Terborg-Penn, 1997). The status of the Black female, in the words of Anna Julia Cooper (1976), is always one that is influenced by the consciousness of representing her community "when and where" she enters. This tradition, a direct descendant of slavery and its ravages, causes Norris (1992) to describe the Black American woman as "the most resilient" among her sisters in the world. Our skin color leaves us vulnerable to the slights and scourges that society metes out to those who are unfortunate enough to bear the marks of their African ancestors. This legacy includes lower wages, less health care, more children living in poverty, a greater likelihood of ending up in jail on minimum charges than their White counterparts, and a minimum level of education (Gregory, 1999).

To be Black and a woman also means that you strive to resist the narrow limits of traditional expectations, for those of your kind, in a country with Eurocentric values. It means that you must continually reach back in history and remember the examples set by women such as Sojourner Truth, Harriet Tubman, Phyllis Wheatley, Fannie Lou Hamer, Septima Clarke, Wilma Rudolf, and Marian Anderson (Igus, 1991). Whether a preacher, teacher, revolutionary, or athlete, all of these women set a standard for excellence that cut across race, class, and national boundaries. And each one of them did their work in a less than supportive environment. In this tradition, the Black woman finds herself pitting her will to survive against the will of a nation that constantly struggles to undo her best efforts, or ignore them.

The pieces of these women's stories can be laid out to show the places where my consciousness of being Black identifies with the symbols of their interface with the United States. I present a "quilt" below that offers some testimony to my "ouch" reaction when I listened to the video testimony of these GED graduates. To some, the pieces that I choose may not be compelling enough, or violent enough, to convince them that I have anything to shout about. To others, I may simply protest too much. But to those with a discerning eye, those with enough experience in the "race game" that is modern America (West, 1994), I believe that they will find enough power in the women's words to hear what I heard and feel as I felt, as I listened to tape after tape of the interviews. Here are the examples:

Regina:

My parents, or I can say my parent, my Dad, lived a pretty wild life. Growing up, he ran a social house and back in the early sixties where they did, I mean, you could come and buy liquor twenty-four hours a day, any kind of drugs you wanted. You could even buy a woman there, you could get your body piercing going on, and you could get your booze. During the early sixties I was too young for him to make me go in and be a part of the business. But he always promised me as a young girl that as soon as I got old enough that I would be a part of the business. He sold everything he could. He sold my mother, and he would beat her after he sold her.

Maria:

I had this thing about talking to certain people. I would only talk to people that I thought was on my level or below me. And people that could inspire me, or could help me or push . . . I never wanted to deal with. I didn't know why but I didn't want to deal with these type people. And until I met Angela and them, and they really pushed me and they took an interest in me, what I did and gave me things to do to show me what I could do, this was my turning point, you know.

## Carmen:

There was so many times this girl had to walk about six or seven miles to get to the bus stop. Much less get to school. . . . she not only had to walk all those miles; she was sitting in this class every day. That woman didn't know how to miss no school. Rain, sleet, or snow.

## Evelyn:

It was too much, I was too embarrassed to go back, it was like I had made the dumbest mistake in the universe, not in the world, but in the universe. Ah, and then I met another guy and I thought that you know . . . I needed to be a little woman then, and my mom used to tell me that "you have done everything that a woman can do," so I felt more of a woman than a child and when I'd see my peers, it was a big difference between us, even though we were the same age, it just seemed like I had crossed over some lines that wouldn't allow me go back.

## Christine:

At some point I did [feel like I had self-esteem problems]; but I always felt like I was the black sheep at home and getting attention the wrong way, I just fed in to that and it just became a part of my life and felt like that was where I fitted in. Really, I was just doing under all the wrong instructions. I was just following people who were leading me down the wrong road because I wanted the attention.

## C.C.:

It's a state where if people start having a conversation, you feel like they're talking over your head; a state where if they sitting down reading a book, you feel strange because you don't have the energy, or the time, or the knowledge to read that same book, you know, and it's depressing, that's the state. And you don't want to be that way; you want to be able to pick up a newspaper and read it and not only read it, but to understand what it's saying to you.

## Michelle:

There was a group of us that used to hang together. And I guess you could say I was the leader. Everybody looked to me for advice. I always dressed nice and was popular. I did okay in school. I never made any F's. I just didn't like school that much with somebody always telling you what to do. And most of it was just busy work. You know. I wasn't really learning anything. I already knew how to count money. And that was all that I was about—business. Anyway we used to cut school a lot, ride the bus to different places, and just hang out. Before you know it, I had not been to school in two weeks. And then when I went, I just didn't feel like I did belong, so I left.

Each time I heard a story about a family that was forced to offer one of its children up as a sacrifice to the great god of "surviving," I could hear the echoes of slave narratives from W.E.B. DuBois' story, *The Souls of Black Folk* (1965). When would we be delivered from that too familiar storyline, I asked myself, so that we could go on to claim our overdue rewards from this unjust society? Would it be possible for me to write passionately about any other topic in this academic environment before the end of the twenty-first century?

When I heard these women talk about the lack of self-esteem that drove them to give up on themselves long before they left high school, I wondered if the tape in my mind was on pause. Didn't I hear this story before? Wasn't it there in Nella Larsen's *Passing* (Larson, 1992)? I could close my eyes and imagine that I was sitting in a room with Sojourner Truth, who never got a formal education but did not let that stop her from achieving her goal in life as a leader of social change. But we got the right to an education, an equal education, in 1954, my mind protests, as I sit with my eyes closed and reflect on our educational history. So how come this woman's story reminds me of the tremendous odds that Jarena Lee encountered when she set about to write the first autobiography of an African-American woman (Andrews, 1986)? "Same old, same old," my conscience retorts. But these are "successful" women who have overcome a huge obstacle in the race to be financially independent and worthy of belonging to the tradition of Black people who have embraced the ethic of education as the topmost priority in the lives of Black people.

And as I "worked the data" to find the excerpts of joy that represented these women's victory over ignorance of the high school-level literacy that is served up in public schools, I found myself getting squeamish about the reality that these women were up against.

Would they make enough money to pay their rent and feed

their children? How many employers would recognize their latent potential, evidenced in their commitment to provide for their families, and give them the opportunity to be leaders at the sites where they were employed? How many managers would allow them the time to leave their jobs, minimum wage jobs, to go back to school so that they would be able to continue the upward climb to another level of academic skill and thus improve their financial and social circumstances? How much hard living could any woman, any person, endure before she found this grinding pursuit of "improvement" too much to contend with on a daily basis?

These are questions that rattled around in my head as I tried to make sense of my reaction to the success stories of these women. They are questions that come up because they are representative of the experiences that I have come to understand through my own journey in the academic world. They are bubbles that float to the top of my agenda for deeper investigation of our ideas about the price that people of color should pay if they want to become visible in this society. I turn up the volume on my inner radio and listen to Ellison remind me of the tale in *The Invisible Man* (1952) and ask myself how much of that can be translated into the story of these Black women? How many more chances will these women be allowed in order to make some progress from the grim challenge of their lives before they come in to sight on the screen that is mainstream America?

Although I have quoted from the nine women's interviews in this introduction, the following pages will highlight the stories of just four of the women. I found these stories to be the most compelling of the nine that we documented. The levels of courage and commitment that these four women—Carmen, Carolee, Maria, and Evelyn—represented seemed symbolic of all of the stories that we were privileged to record. In each case the reader will find a clear example of personal growth and a unique display of personal accountability in the face of the country's seeming indifference to the reality of being Black, female, poor, and talented.

TWO

# Carmen Montana

Carmen Montana's best friend from grade-school days, Ann, recalls that "when [Carmen] was a young girl she couldn't go to school because of being sick, you know, a lot of days." Asthma accounted for Montana's intermittent attendance at school before she dropped out.

When Carmen Montana was sixteen, she walked out of school because she was not given permission to study general business in the ninth grade. She ended up with a lot of time on her hands and that led her to drinking and "messing around" with people who didn't "mean her any good."

Once she walked out of school she had different reasons for staying away from her formal education. Montana says that she spent her time at "clubs and nightclubs and movies and things like that," which did not mean anything of value to her.

When word got around to the mother of a friend of hers that Montana was not going to school and that she was spending a lot of time "drinking and going to clubs and bars and such," the friend's mother decided to take action.

Montana recalls that the woman began:

> Talking to me about church or God or whatever, which I couldn't quite understand a lot about then. But she was very effective, you know, she talked to me and she really got my mind, you know, somehow what she said to me, and she had prayer with me and all that stuff, something about that turned me around.

Once Montana began attending church on a regular basis, she became committed to her new way of life. She remembers that she began to:

Teach Sunday school and things of that nature, and I began to do public speaking then. Even in church I was bringing messages at that point. That's when I began to feel like I need to learn more about the *Bible*, that's when I enrolled in the Bible college courses and stuff, you know, and began to learn more how to teach the *Bible*, that's how I started.

Bible college represented a commitment to study and be tested on the scripture and analysis of the verses. Montana studied with a group of people who helped her memorize verses, and learn to explain the meanings of words and ideas from the Bible. She also developed a style of presenting the written answers to the test questions. Testing at the Bible college often involved multiple-choice questions or choosing the correct name for a king after reading a description of the events that the king was involved with. Other times the test would ask you to fill in blanks that were scattered throughout several verses from the week's scripture lesson. The written part of the tests would ask questions like "What are the four types of love?" or require an explanation of a quotation, such as, "Wait on the Lord and be of good courage." These were graded for correctness of answer more than adequacy of written expression.

The decision to attend Bible college brought many rewards to Montana. Having stayed in the church through her late teens and into her thirties, she accumulated a lot of experience as a speaker. Presenting sermons in church and teaching Sunday school became part of her life story. When Montana talks about the way in which Bible college prepared her for the discipline of the General Educational Diploma (GED) program, she recalls the benefits of spiritual training by emphasizing that "the Bible is needed, you need to be strong, you need good character," if you are going to succeed as a student.

Montana also explains that she:

> Went to Bible college to be able to speak more effectively. Know how to use the words, know how to tell the stories, know how to put what in what text, that was good ... it's one of the great things in life that a minister or speaker need to do if they can afford it, or have an opportunity.

The result of this spiritual training is acknowledged by Montana's friends and family. The strength of her character is referred to many times when her best friend, Ann, speaks of her:

She's really saying something when she talks, you know somebody gets up and they just make, use a lot of words, but she, she got a point to bring out. And when she brings it out, you know, we are all encouraged by what she's saying.

In Montana's estimation:

The word of God tells you to learn how to dwell with the people in this world. That's saying a whole lot. That's saying, go to school so you can do well, get your education so you won't be kicked down, you know. Learn how to live among them, live peaceable among them, that's what the Bible says.

Once Montana began delivering messages in the church, she became aware of her "gift." When she talks about the way in which she is inspired to choose topics, she shows her spiritual culture:

Most of your messages are inspired or anointed by God. You just feel it. It's something, you feel the anointing coming on you, you know, to speak on a subject. And most all the subjects I ever spoke on, that's how I received it, by inspirational receiving. It's just not something I just think up.

This ability to divine the level on which to reach people also influences the way in which Montana ministered to her congregation. Her description of the encounters that she had with prostitutes shows how Montana has been able to bring her life experience into her work. She recalls,

I put my arms around [the prostitute] and I just talked to her, I told her you don't have to be this way. They don't have to sleep out and be drunk and having hangovers . . . After I got through telling her that I was in the street one day, you know, I used to drink, I used to sleep around, but I said I stopped that, got myself a good husband, children.

Montana's stories of "uplift" also include one about her own family. In this recollection she describes a victory over her older sister's degrading lifestyle:

I went and got my own sister. She was a drunk, she was an alcoholic . . . She'll be so drunk I don't even know how she could hold her cup . . . I don't even know how she went to work next morning. She had a common-law husband, drunk, going down, I say for the last count . . .

I hung in there, I stayed there . . . That little thing [finally] straighten her life out.

Before Carmen Montana began her GED program she was involved in several literacy activities that related to the business of conducting her life. She read all of the books that her children had to use in school. Her oldest daughter, Maria, was in the seventh grade when Montana decided to return to school. At that time Montana was particularly helpful with the Math, English, Science, and Social Studies homework exercises that the children were assigned for school.

Montana was also a poet who would pen special verses for her friends and family on special occasions like their birthdays or anniversaries. She would let the person who received the poem learn "what I think and who you really are" in the verses. Her best friend, Ann, has saved many of these poems over the years. For entertainment Montana would read novels by her favorite author, Grace Livingston Hill. The themes that attracted her had to do with people "searching for happiness in life" and people in low circumstances "trying to overcome" their situation. The other books that Montana would read included stories about someone's life "going downhill and then someone would turn it around."

Since Montana loves to cook, she always collected recipes and shared them with her family and friends. She has a collection of her favorite recipes and the ones that people often ask her to share. Ann says that Montana "collects recipes like some women collect lipstick." According to Ann, Montana always has a scrap of paper in her pocketbook with ingredients scribbled on the back.

In the twenty-five years that Montana has been involved in preaching sermons, she evolved a plan for writing an outline. Her notes would include "the subject, the main thoughts, and a conclusion." She would use the outline to help her think out the logic of her sermon and select the verses of scripture that she wanted to use in her lesson. Although the outline would be fairly brief and take about a page, it would supply her with enough thoughts to conduct the sermon for more than an hour. Some of the titles of her sermons included: "Now Faith Is . . . (fill in the blank)"; "Do you know Him?" and "Seven Steps to Victory."

Montana was also involved in teaching Sunday school and being the secretary for the Sunday school committee before she entered the GED program. She enjoys both jobs very much and was always happy to write the minutes as part of her duties in the church. For Vacation Bible School she would plan three lessons for every week that the children were under her supervision. Ever aware that she should not "crowd a child's mind," Montana would choose stories about important men like David, the three Hebrew brothers, and Moses, and plan activities around these subjects. Montana would also plan to do craft projects like making lighthouses out of poster board, or creating picture frames and aquariums with painted fish in them.

Montana was also able to help one member of her congregation prepare for the driver's license exam. She would read the rules from the book and have the man memorize the answers. She also taught him "to identify the signs by the shape and the colors." Montana created small tests for the man and had him answer her without any prompting. The man was eventually able to sit for the oral exam for his license and then go on to apply for a job where he could drive. Without Montana's help he would not have been able to find a job that would adequately provide for his family.

Montana came to the GED program with at least an eighth-grade reading level, an understanding of the Bible, and vocabulary from the novels that she was reading and discussing at the time. The task in the GED classroom would be learning what she missed in the ninth- to twelfth-grade years.

With all her gifts of expression, it was still important to Montana to complete her high school education. She remembers that "maybe when I was about forty and I got to thinking, you know, when I put my children in school, I realized there was things I know and things I didn't know."

Montana's reasons for deciding to return to school can best be addressed by reviewing the changes that took place in her relationship with her children and their schoolwork. The five children ranged in ages from eight to thirteen. Her oldest child is Maria, then there is a boy, then a boy and a girl who are twins, and the youngest child is a girl.

In our first interview the proud mother was able to say: "To see what they had to do, the things were so new to me, I wanted to go back to school myself."

Her friend, Joyce, has a similar view of the reasons that Montana had for returning to school. In her analysis: "I could tell that, you know, maybe like her children and their schoolwork, she maybe didn't feel like she was capable of helping them with their work."

Montana's sister, Jane, remembers that Montana did not talk to her children much and the result was that the children did not have a lot of opportunity to express themselves at home. Jane says that their vocabulary was not very well developed. Ann, her childhood friend, also feels that Montana did not feel capable of helping her children with their assignments and projects for school.

Mrs. Montana's Sunday school supervisor and friend, Joyce, also attests to the restlessness in her church sister and suggests that "she had a lot of knowledge within herself at that point. But yet she needed, you know, the GED experience to bring it out of her." Her childhood friend, Ann, echoes the same sentiment when she reflects that "[Montana] can be smart, but you have to have somebody to teach you how to use your smartness, and where to put it" and Montana's aim in going back to school was to learn how to be more "outspoken in her church."

Maria, her eighth-grade daughter, also feels that her mother believed that a better education would put Montana in a position to improve the quality of life that the family was experiencing. With a better education would come better instruction in the Bible, better help with homework, maybe a better home and neighborhood, and a mother who was better able to provide for the future of her children both physically and spiritually.

She also had a better understanding of the world and the need for a good job.

> You can tell that [merchant] all you want to, that your faith going to get this paid for, your faith is not. You got to get that man some Lincolns, some Jacksons, see what I'm saying, and Washingtons. That's five dollar bills and twenty dollar bills and hundred dollar bills. That's what he's looking at to pay your light bill.

This pragmatic view of life led Montana to talk with Joyce about her idea of a business. Miss Zeely, Montana's role model, says that Montana loves to cook and see people enjoy her food, so she has always had this dream of owning her own bed and breakfast inn. Joyce recounts that they "talked about how to go about getting a loan, how to go about finding the house and then from what, you know, what to do from there."

Maria also recounts the plans that her mother has shared with her concerning the bed and breakfast inn:

> She says she will let me work there maybe as a waitress, or a person that comes in there and cleans up the rooms and she will let me get paid for it and everything. She wants her sister to open . . . a restaurant next to it, so you just walk across to get something to eat. That's a good idea, it would make quite a bit of money.

Ann remembers that the business was always "a dream of hers, you know, that one day she will open a bed and breakfast of her own."

In her folder from the year of the GED program Montana keeps several copies of the sayings and quotes that she collected over the nine months of her studies. Her favorite saying, printed on bright pink paper with black ink, is the one that she believes describes her journey and attitude. It states that "The measure of a woman is the size of the problem that it takes to stop her!" Montana was not stopped by a broken leg, asthma attacks, or her mother's death. Nor was she discouraged by the lack of direction that her classmates displayed at times.

When Montana arrived at the women's center for her GED classes, she would usually be the first one in the classroom. She worked alone until the rest of the class and the teacher arrived. Then they would all do a "brain twister" together for the opening exercise. This activity would allow all the students to work to their individual strengths as they contributed to finding the right answer to the question. The Math, Language Arts and Literature, Science, Reading Comprehension, and Social Studies curricula that she studied were "very enlightening."

Montana found the Social Studies course was her favorite subject because "it was telling me about the world and how to live in it." Montana claims that as a result of the program, she "can look at the news, understand things I once didn't, understand people speaking, they can talk about things [in] any part of the world." The whole course of study allowed her to become more effective with helping her children in their learning. As she stated in our first interview:

I helped [my children] write essays, write their reports, Math, and I understand, you know, better how to help my children. My speeches are better because I know how to form the essay. I know how to prepare my topic; I know how to get my conclusion. And I know what goes in between, you know. And so it helped me when I started to give a speech. It kind of organized my speech in other words.

She also had a special interest in Math because she wanted to learn to balance her checkbook. Her teacher taught her how to do it and observed that "the only problem that she had with balancing a checkbook was that she didn't have one. It was not something that was very complicated for her."

Montana found herself in a special role in this group of adult students. Because she was one of the advanced readers, she was given the responsibility of working with students who needed additional support with their studies. The teacher also encouraged Montana to instruct the class on some days so that she could get the experience of talking to an audience that was different from her congregation. To promote her involvement in the class exercises, since she was working at a higher level than most of the other students, the GED teacher told Montana that "she was helping [herself and] . . . the other students" by acting as a role model.

Olivia, the GED teacher, refers to the group sharing as an important part of the learning process in which these women engaged. When the women heard each other's life stories, since it was only women in the group, it allowed them to open up and find support from the students who formerly struggled with similar problems. It also created a bond between the women that helped them feel a sense of belonging that they would otherwise not have in their lives. Olivia observed that "the closeness among the members is very important when women have so many outside conflicts."

During the afternoon session the students would work on their individual reading programs or concentrate on a subject that they wanted to practice doing on their own. Montana would always choose algebra as her subject for the afternoon. She would always try

> To crack little problems, or solve a problem and figure out what root I would come up, what number, you know. That's what I enjoyed. I loved the negative and positives of the problem. And seem like when I get in the negative of the problem . . . that's when it becomes the most challenging.

Montana was also very good at spelling and got perfect marks on all the spelling tests. The women were also given a lot of opportunity to write on topics suggested by the GED teacher, such as famous people or personal experiences. Montana remembers that her first essay was about Shirley Chisholm. She got an A grade for the essay and lamented that she did not get an A+ since she did not do any indentation. Montana was very proud about that essay because she had not written in that style for at least thirty-two years. She was also proud about the fact that one of her essays on a pet dog, Snowball, was chosen to represent the class on a public notice board outside of the school's administrative offices.

### The Impact of Montana's GED

To understand the true value of the GED in Montana's life, one has to consider the tremendous implications of her literacy growth on her family. They understood that Montana was far more educated than the GED certificate indicated. They looked to the successful completion of the GED as an indicator of different levels of growth in Montana and her social network's life.

Two of Montana's friends, Ann and Joyce, can only speculate about the effect of the GED certificate on the relationship between Mr. and Mrs. Montana. But Jane, Montana's sister, says that she sees a marked difference in her sister's husband. She notes that "they have become closer to each other and he has changed a whole lot, [he has] grown closer to the children, they do more together, and [Montana] can depend on him more."

Montana appreciates the way that her husband supported her effort to achieve her GED certificate and she applauds his attitude to her as the "speaker" of the house. She says that she is the one who does all the negotiating with the children's schoolteachers and the businessmen who have to handle the Montanas' affairs. Now that the GED certificate is in Montana's possession, however, Jane says that Mr. Montana "sees a different and better person and he depends on her more now than he did back then." It seems to Jane that Mr. Montana is "doing more for her now than he did before she went back to school."

Ann, Montana's best friend, saw Mr. Montana do his utmost to be a family man during the nine-month vigil toward the GED certificate. Now she believes that her friend's spouse "is very proud of [Montana] also, and he has . . . a whole lot of confidence in her that she'll make something of herself and be just whatever she set out to be."

Montana will tell you from the first time that you meet her and begin talking about school that she has been a light to those in her church and her GED class. When her children encouraged her to announce at a church function that she had received her GED certificate, Montana stood up and explained to the congregation: "Don't drop out. Don't. Cause like I say, you the one that going to regret it. Cause I am . . . forty-nine, and I have regret it for dropping out." The positive effect of this cautionary tale on the elder members of the church represents Montana's credibility with her congregation. Several people have begun discussing plans to return to school. Her sister admitted that "there's a lot of us that haven't finished school and you know, a person that age going back to finish school, it give everybody, you know, something to think about."

The "predicament" of not having a high school education keeps rearing its head when Montana's friends discuss the meaning of her achievement in the context of her work as a minister as well. As far as Miss Zeely, the choir director at the church, is concerned, "she may be a light in the tunnel to somebody else. We don't know that yet but that may . . . come out a year later."

Montana herself supports the view that her struggle has an effect on the people around her. She knows that "when you go on you can encourage someone else . . . because your life don't only affect you it affect whoever is around." Further proof of that philosophy is in the fact that Miss Zeely believes that Montana is a good model for the youth in the church. When the young people look at the aspiring minister they see that "you don't have to stay in the same situation that you're in, you don't have to feel sorry for yourself," according to Miss Zeely.

The continually widening circle of Montana's influence is further informed by her newly acquired political voice. Montana's reaction to the state's decision to cut the number of GED classes at the women's center where she studied for her GED certificate resulted in a letter to the senator in charge. If the school programs are withdrawn, then Montana will be crippled in her fight to get the "down and outs" with the "up and in."

As Montana says:

> I can hear what is being said [by the senator] to my generation and the generation after me. I see it and I hear it. And I'm fighting right now to let the people see if we don't save [the adult education programs] now they are not going to be saved.

The effect of Montana's increased literacy skills on her students in Sunday school, her sister, and her friends can be traced in the references that they make to their observations of how she functions in her usual jobs. In Sunday school, Montana's supervisor has observed the new way that the lessons have been structured for the young children. There is a system of presenting the stories from the Bible when the children give a summary of the day's lesson to the church. If Montana was teaching about Zachariah she would "have pictures of trees and telling the students about different kinds of trees and what the significance of the tree was and what it was doing," according to Joyce. Montana would also "ask each [child] a question about what was taught" before going on to do some kind of artwork.

Montana's sister Jane has also found that she is more likely to call on her aspiring minister sister if she cannot understand the passage that she is studying from the Bible. "I can call her and she says, "well wait a minute" and she gets her Bible and explains the words Jane has trouble with. Jane also testifies that the GED classes "gave her a more variety of words and things to use that she didn't know at first to use."

This fact is also mentioned by Montana's daughter, Maria, when she observes that her mother "explained things well before she got her GED, and now she explains them more elaborate [and] it comes in handy, cause if she ever goes to a job interview, she use them big words, they might give her a job just cause they don't know what in the world she talking about."

In Maria's estimation, the job that her mother would get as a result of her increased literacy level would also lead to a better housing district, better schools for her siblings, and the possibility of college for all the children.

THREE

# Carolee Carpenter

Carolee Carpenter, who goes by the nickname C.C., began her GED journey as part of the custodial staff at First State University. Her decision to join the newly formed literacy class at the university was the result of a long struggle with her negative self-concept. This attitude, based on her level of literacy training, resulted in her being in a "depressing state" and having low self-esteem. She remembered that the first intimations of panic about her educational status began when her children were in the fourth and fifth grades. The realization that they were learning things very different from what she had mastered at their age, and that her oldest friend's daughter could "read better" and faster than she could, intimidated her to the point that she kept longing to do better for herself. After thinking about making a change and talking about the need to do something for herself, she got the courage that "reality" delivered to her when she made up her mind that it was time to do something. As she stated:

> Reality pushes you through the door . . . You wake up one morning and you know [that] you talked about it, you planned on it, but you have yet to do anything about it and you have to give up and put your first foot forward and start to work on it.

Besides the fact that her children were bringing home more difficult homework than she could assist them with, C.C. also found it difficult to keep up with her tasks at work because she could not read all of the materials that she had to handle on the job. Like other workers on the job, she thought that people "should be able to read the chemicals—it would prevent accidents from happening because you could read [and you] don't have to depend on your memory."

She began attending literacy classes at First State University during the day even though she was working on the night shift. Eventually, though, her schedule changed and she was able to begin attending classes while she was a regular day worker. She even enlisted at Literacy, Inc. because it was close to First State University where she worked. With this added boost to her study time, she began the long journey to success in all parts of the GED exam.

At one time in her life before she achieved enough points to earn the GED diploma, C.C. remembered wanting to give up. She failed the test three times and had to do the separate parts at different times before scoring the right points. Her grown children kept reminding her: "you could do it, it' s going to be a little hard, it's been a long time since you studied, but it'll all start coming back to you." She also had the support of her GED teacher, who took a personal interest in each of the students and made sure that she knew a good deal of their background in order to motivate them when things got to be a challenge. She would tell them "work on this [test] ten minutes and then do what you want to do," as a way to get people out of their negative mood. And most times the students would spend a lot longer on the test, to their benefit.

C.C. also remembers the following important aspect about the literacy class that she belonged to:

> It helps motivate you and knowing what you want and the way you got to get it and that somebody there that cared, who is going to be there for you, waiting on you to come in with your books on the table, ready to help you.

Most important, C.C. had come to a point in her life where she realized that she had to do the exam for herself, not her children, or her teacher, or her boss, or the students in the class who were studying with her. "You can't do it for no one else," she explained. "If you not doing it for yourself, then no need in wasting your time because the only person that is worthy of doing it for, is yourself." This turning point in her attitude to the exam and what it represented in her life helped to push her over the obstacle of a lack of self-esteem and onward to the place where she was able to celebrate her victory over the formidable odds of self-doubt.

When she reflects on her journey toward obtaining the GED diploma, she describes it as a "tornado" because she never knew "which way the wind would blow" her. She was excited by the challenge of the reading and writing tasks, especially when she had to learn to read maps and do math, but it always made her feel "afraid" because everything about it was new. C.C. also remembers that there was some jealousy among a few of the people in the GED class when she passed different parts of the exam. She thinks that this was a good thing for some people because it motivated them to work harder and achieve their individual goals. Also, because the class was fairly close, she was able to bring back her experience of working on the tests to the group and encourage people to keep on pushing until they were able to pass the battery of tests. She would tell them to:

> Make sure that you have your multiplications, your additions and your subtractions down pat and if you miss one part of it, you'll still be done [with] a great deal of it enough to pass . . . and you can always go back and learn what you didn't learn, you still got time to do that.

Since passing the GED exam, C.C. has moved on from a custodial 1 staff position to a superintendent position over a large area of First State University. This new job puts her in a supervisory position over the custodial staff, the very people she once worked alongside. She graduated from custodial 1 to level 3 and then to foreman, supervisor, and finally superintendent in a few years. While she wanted, and worked for the position of foreman, her promotion to superintendent was entirely fortuitous. She had actually refused her boss's offer of the new job and told him "I don't know about that." After two people failed to meet the demands of the job, it became clear that she could handle the new responsibilities that she was once fearful of assuming.

What has been most challenging to her in her new role as a GED graduate? She believes that the responsibility for people and paperwork would have to be listed at the top of her concerns. She works to treat the custodial staff in the way that she wanted to be treated when she was in that position. "You try to let people know that . . . I'm here with you and whatever we're in, we're in it together," she explains.

At one time she wanted to write up a staff member for some infraction on the job and her supervisor encouraged her to counsel the worker rather than file a complaint. She drafted a letter and rewrote it according to her boss's directions and then delivered the letter to the worker. As she recounts this incident, she realizes that it was a learning experience for her because she had to use the literacy skills that she had acquired in the GED class and be willing to ask for help from her boss. Both activities made her aware that she was capable of meeting new demands on her skills and that she would not have had the courage to face the situation before the GED diploma. She also realized that she was developing interpersonal skills that would not have been necessary before she embarked on the GED path.

During the journey to the superintendent position that she held when we did her series of interviews, C.C. also discovered that many of the people in similar positions were not infallible. Her perception of workers in "street clothes," which represented their senior rank over the custodians, changed when she found mistakes on paperwork that was processed by senior staff. Once she understood that anyone could make a mistake, she became less demanding of herself when she attempted new tasks. She also became appreciative of the level of persistence that she had acquired through her struggle to increase her level of literacy while she was a member of the GED class. This kind of determination paid off in the fact that she had acquired the habit of "checking behind" herself when she did new tasks, to be sure that they were correctly completed. She also realized that other people around her appreciated her for her ability to commit to and complete a task in the face of the odds that presented themselves because they were new and/or difficult.

Once she began the climb up the career ladder at First State University, she had to adjust to the demands that it made on her life at home. For a while she would take the work troubles home, and let the home situation affect her attitude at work. Slowly she came to accept that this approach to her new life was not working in her favor. Now she leaves her work at the university, even if her coworkers feel free to call her when she has returned home after a long day at work. She leaves her home life at the house, so that it does not affect her attitude to the workers that she has to supervise on the job. She once felt that her husband expected her to change for the worse when she got her promotion to superintendent, but she proved that fear to be misplaced. It is important to her to "remember where you come from" and treat people the way you want to be treated, "then everything works out."

Now that there is less concern about "money for clothes, money for food" and other necessities, C.C. is thinking about going to college. Her children, all of whom have gone to college, tell people that their mother is going to continue with her education. C.C. smiles when she reports this attitude of her children because she knows how proud her accomplishment with the GED made them. She also knows that her mother was completely supportive of her ambitions during the GED journey. A return to school would be a dream come true, C.C. reports, but she wants to give something to her job because it has been so good to her. Without the free classes on the campus, C.C. would not have been able to achieve her educational goals. She wants to be there for other workers who decide to improve themselves through education and to inspire them to work hard through her example as a product of an increased level of literacy.

Talking about the GED journey causes C.C. to compare the experience to being at a high school prom. The feeling of excitement pervades her attitude and body language as she talks about the meaning of the GED in her life. She believes that the GED is a symbol of "self-confidence" and that she would encourage anyone who wanted to do the battery of tests to make time for themselves. "Whatever I do in life I got to put me first. It's more important than anything. I have to make sure that I'm happy," she says. This is an important message to her and others whom she works with on the campus. After your children are grown, she says, "you have to find something to do with yourself." When you look around and see what a good job you have done with your children, she adds, you tell yourself that it's time to do something "wonderful" for yourself.

The decision to do something for herself led her to face her great fear of change. She had to stop telling herself that she could not "remember" anything. She had to keep telling herself to continue going to classes when she did not make enough points to pass each section of the GED. She had to insist that she expect better for herself when no one on the job seemed to notice that she was struggling with depression and the shame that her children were enjoying a better lifestyle than she did because they had gone to college and she had not finished high school. These feelings of being inadequate sometimes made her want to withdraw from people and conversations where she did not feel she could understand the language or subject that the group was discussing. She remembers "hear[ing] those young people saying things that [I] couldn't really pronounce, words that [I] couldn't pronounce and you know that you just go to change, you don't want your kids to see you in this state."

Looking back on the journey to her present improved circumstances, C.C. feels that there was more to the GED journey than getting the right score to earn the diploma. She insists that the constant feeling that people "were looking down" on her was entirely due to her feelings about her inadequacies. Once she achieved her long-sought goal, she no longer felt those negative things about herself. People around her began celebrating her victories in other areas of life. She came to realize that her thinking patterns were based on her lack of self-appreciation. Further, she came to accept how much her children wanted her to be successful in this literacy goal. It was their insistent voices reminding her that she could succeed that made her believe that they felt she was a capable woman and thinker. Once she accepted that they saw her victory as their personal achievement, she was inspired to continue her self-development in other areas.

C.C. has attained such a high level of self-confidence and expects such positive outcomes in her life that she describes her new attitude in these words:

> You start to thinking positive and acting positive and you want to do things and you may just find yourself in the kitchen preparing dinner and you are just singing where you never found yourself singing before, and you just feel good and you have that energy that you didn't have before because you got self-confidence.

The feeling is very different from the depressive state that she used to live with before she embarked on the GED journey. She knows that she has won a major victory over self-doubt and proven to her most severe critic, herself, that she can meet a challenge and come out victorious.

As she explained:

> You just wake up in the morning saying you ready to go, cause you know what you going to do when you get to work, you are going to go to work . . . and you [are] ready to go.

Every new task that she completes on the job leads her to a new level of self-appreciation. She takes on new challenges with a gusto that comes from having succeeded before and the knowledge that there are people who will support her as she grows in expertise in her field.

How does the GED training show up on her job? She does payroll, she has to "add up the hours" that people work on the job, and that means using all the math that she learned during her class time on campus. When she was studying for the math exam on the GED, she told herself that all she needed to earn was the minimum points to get through the exam. Now she realizes that she is using all the knowledge that she acquired during the training sessions leading up to the math exam.

She also uses her writing skills to do letters and complete the paperwork that her supervisory position creates. This means that she has to apply the grammar and punctuation rules that were so tedious to learn during the time that she was struggling to succeed with the battery of tests. Overall, her level of awareness of the demands on the superintendent is informed by the fact that she has mastered the ability to express herself. This consciousness came as a direct result of her learning to apply herself to the task of the GED coursework with a singular devotion to the mastery of the new material. She brings the discipline of this focused attention to the new tasks that come to her on the job or at her home. As she explained:

> When the door open[s], you feel joy. You feel afraid because you don't know what's ahead, but you know whatever it is, you are going to conquer it. If you going to get what you need, you got to conquer it, and then once you have completed that journey, you realize that it was worth everything you been through.

FOUR

# Maria Walters

When Maria left high school in 1975, she had no idea that she would return to high school after working in a textile mill for six years. Then a high school junior, an athlete, and known to be "bright" because she was an honor roll student, she was also pregnant and determined to have her child, whose father was a player on the basketball team. She was very good at the jobs that she did at the mill, but one day she looked at an old woman who had worked there for thirty years and she made up her mind to change her life. The woman had a hump on her back "from changing machines, rolling corn, and other stuff," and had never done any other work in her whole life. It was enough for Maria, who "learned very quickly and was a productive worker," to go up to Technical College and register for the GED program.

Maria remembers her years at the textile mill as a very productive learning opportunity. She learned the various jobs quickly, she "taught other people how to do [her] job," and was on her way to being the supervisor of her shift. In fact, she "would run circles around the other people and quickly made a name for herself." Something in her, though, told her that she could do better for herself and her baby daughter. She had a car, she was dating a new friend, and she knew that she had crossed over into a new life that her old friends from high school were not going to understand. Maria realized that her "potential was greater" than she was allowing herself to experience by working at the mill. As she recalls this transition period, she explains her belief that "someone can tell you that life isn't a bed of roses, but when you learn for yourself that it really isn't and it's up to you . . . the kind of garden that you make for yourself." She had to come to the decision to pursue a higher ideal on her own time.

Although it may be true that some people see the GED as a "negative," Maria says that it is a very positive experience in her life. Her understanding of her personal and academic development following the achievement of the GED are reflected in her analysis of her early years after high school. She saw herself as the "breadwinner" at home, and had taken on the responsibility of raising her younger siblings because her mother was gone a lot. Her father, on the other hand, was the one person who continually reminded her that it was "not too late" to return to school and further her education. She remembers meeting a former student at the high school after this classmate had completed college and remarking to herself that "if she went to college, even the time that you have been out, you should be able to go back and do something with your life." The girl, Maria says, was not "one of the brighter kids" in high school.

When Maria finally made time to do the assessment test at the GED office, she found out that she could begin classes and basically arrange the schedule to suit herself. This suited her fine because she was now on second shift and her grandmother and sister were helping her with her daughter. The most attractive part about the new school arrangement was the fact that the classes were held at Technical College, so people thought that Maria was attending college. Only her family knew that she was doing the GED program, and they were proud of her. "I had to do it somewhere outside of people knowing what was really happening with me," she says. Maria believed that the college campus "aroused [her interest in school] more" because people thought that she was back in school.

Maria sees this time in her life as the chance for her to "redevelop as a person" because she "needed to feel the halls of learning again, because it was something that was lost in my mind." It was also an "esteem builder" and made her realize that "every mistake is not a mistake." Since she saw herself as a "provider" for her family, and felt an "obligation" to her four siblings, she knew that she was setting a precedent for the younger children. Her older sister did not finish high school, and her mother thought that Maria "made her bed" and therefore she should "lie in it," an attitude that did not make it easy for her daughter to continue with her educational plans.

In one month, to her teacher's surprise, Maria was ready to do the GED exam. Her teacher, who thought that she would do well, insisted that Maria try the full battery of tests even though Maria was concerned about her math score. Maria, a young mother, passed the whole test the first time: she made 240 points when she only needed 225 points, and signed up for the nursing program at Technical College. The local newspaper made a big deal about the first GED graduate being accepted to the program and this made the beginning of Maria's college life even more exciting for the promise that it represented. After two years in the nursing program, she decided that nursing was "too much." Fortunately, she was already taking business classes, so she decided to continue on that path and complete her associate's degree in business.

All of this activity was going on while Maria continued to be the mother figure in her family. Her oldest sister, who "was never successful in school," chose to marry when she was fifteen years old. That older sister saw her success as a wife and mother. Her younger brother, on the other hand, was encouraged to finish high school and go to college. In fact, Maria worked two jobs to make sure that he had the financial support to pursue his career in college. She did not want him to leave high school, work at the mill, join the credit union, get a car, and then tell himself that he was a "success." In the small town where they lived, these goals were considered worthy, but not for Maria. Maria wanted more for her brother and was determined to set an example for him by completing her business degree and moving up on the economic ladder.

After eight years working in a finance company, Maria decided that she was not achieving her potential. She had to do a lot of traveling on her job and she was exposed to some of the underhanded business practices that were used against Black people. These clients turned to Maria and her company for financial services. She remembers that "it just seemed like my race of people were being talked to and all kinds of threats [were] being made against their assets that we really knew couldn't happen." She saw herself encouraging people to pay their bills and repeatedly told them to rest assured that their assets were safe. More important, Maria "felt like [she] was helping people," and it was in this role that she began to experience her connection to the community and the need to serve people.

During this stint in the financial company, Maria was involved with the Boys and Girls Club of America on a regular basis after serving a term with that group during a summer program. It was this experience as a teacher, when she began to feel attracted to the role that she played in the lives of children from different backgrounds, that helped her make the decision to return to school and get a teaching degree at Witney College. Maria remembers that:

> I felt like I wanted to be a teacher because I spent the summer prior to [entering college] working with Boys and Girls Club of America. And I realized it was something about teaching made me feel good. It made me open up and it just seemed that I had found my place. So, I decided to go back.

Even though she was twenty years older than the students in those education classes, it did not deter her from achieving her goals. "Teaching is ministry," says Maria, and that's why she feels so responsible for the children in her care.

Further, according to Maria, a public school teacher with five years' experience when interviewed, "if you do [teaching] the "right" way, you shouldn't be able to do it more than ten years." Because she looks for the children who remind her of herself she is always aware of the role that she can play in the development of young children. Part of her preparation to work with children taught her a lot about the importance of good role models in the life of young people. She recounted how she developed her philosophy of teaching early in her career:

> I listened to stories the [children] would tell about teachers and I made up my mind consciously that I never want to say things like this because I'm sure that teachers can't see the hurt afterwards or the damage that's done.

Her goal with her students is to "make a serious difference in their lives." She remembers one child especially, D. J., because he named her as his "best friend" after he was taken from his father and put in a foster home.

D. J. taught her the value of her role as a teacher and to this day she believes that teaching is a "spiritual calling."

In 2000, Maria reported that she had already been named Teacher of the Year after working in the public school system in her city for five years. As a seventh-grade Language Arts teacher, she had published two books and was working on the "third and fourth at the same time." The books were *Seasons*, a collection of spiritual/religious poems about the various stages of her walk with God and *Lord, Why Do I Keep Choosing The Wrong Man?*, a semi-autobiographical novella about her quest for the perfect mate. Her husband, the father of five of her six children, was a graduate of Slate University and a coproducer of plays that Maria wrote. Since his degree is in Family Theater, they decided to start a business together because their interests are complementary. This new chapter in Maria's life is a result of her husband's returning to school at age forty-two in order to obtain his college degree. Maria sees his success as one of the best examples of the power of the GED in her life. Because she completed high school and went on to pursue her studies in college, she set an example for her family. Her struggle to complete two degrees is always used as a reference point when she counsels her children and other members of her family. She wanted her children and her sibling to understand her determination to get an education, and that even though she "fell from the trophy case, [she] was still a trophy."

Maria's oldest daughter has shown the benefit of her mother's example as the first person in the family to graduate. Michelle had the pleasure of going to college at the same time as her mother. Maria was a senior in college when Michelle was a freshman in another program. Michelle, who was the cause of her mother's leaving high school early, was also the inspiration for Maria's determination to finish teacher's college ahead of her oldest child. They made it a "competition" to get good grades and to study hard so that they would always be ahead of the classes in which they were enrolled. Maria remembers these days in college with a lot of pleasure because her oldest daughter had become a "girlfriend" who shared her dreams for a college degree.

The proud mother was also able to share the "dumb mistakes" she had made early in life and get Michelle to understand that she didn't "have to go down the same long, lonesome road" as her mother and take almost two decades to finish college. Maria has worked hard to make her children understand that making up the lost time can take years to get back on track. Many times it was this camaraderie that inspired Maria to stay on the education journey when the heartaches of failing tests and wanting the college training to be over with preoccupied her and made her "equate it with [her] dropout years."

Maria recounted these memories:

> The biggest part about it that I think both of us can appreciate the most, is the part where we understood that even though we were competing, it wasn't about a true competition, it was about each other's success. And there were times when I would fail a test and I would go home and I was like "God, I just can't get it.". . . But by the same token there were some engineering classes that were a headache for her and when she called, I can remember being able to sympathize with her.

The list of achievements among Maria's three oldest daughters is inspiring to anyone who believes in the value of education. Michelle has an Engineering degree. The second oldest child, Anita, has a master's degree in Microbiology. Anita also runs a class for students in the dropout prevention program at the university she attends. Her mother says that this second daughter "understands the importance of a program and she goes out of her way to be a mentor to students who are at risk." The third girl, Yvette, was a junior at Slate University when these interviews were conducted. Maria sees Yvette as the one who benefited most from the college experiences of herself and the two older daughters. They "know where to find the free stuff" she explained, as she talked about the hurdles that students have to jump in order to get financial aid for their studies. Yvette also has the advantage of hearing the accumulated wisdom of the three older women in the household when it comes to studying for the Regency Exam, a college-level reading exam, and always being prepared for class. The mother and older siblings took the fear out of going to college because they had gone before her and succeeded.

Two of Maria's nephews were waiting to hear their GED scores when she told us her story. They were "excited about it" and, for Maria, that represented the importance of the GED in the life of so many young people. She thinks that her life after the GED helped to put her nephews on a road that would lead them to make an effort to improve their lot after high school. Maria believes that "it was encouraging for them to go and be a part of [the program] and know that if they worked hard, if they gave of themselves, that they were going to get a diploma." The GED, according to Maria, is an opportunity for people who have had to make different choices than high school. For whatever the reason, Maria insists, a person can do the GED and continue to build his or her dreams with the assurance that one can make up for lost time, or just get on track for a better life.

Whatever the reason for a person's dropping out of high school, Maria observes, "you really need to go back and work on it, and know that there are people to work with you until you are ready for it, no matter how long it takes, that's a big plus." She "takes her cap off" to the GED because it opens doors that would otherwise be closed to many people. "A diploma is not a lot, but you have to have it" in order to get ahead in life, Maria adds. The old days of getting a job without a high school diploma, or settling for a job in the textile mill, Maria says, are long gone.

As far as a support system in her life during the passage from GED graduate to public schoolteacher, Maria feels that her baby sister was the most consistent and appreciative person around her. This sister has since returned to school at age thirty-nine to do her GED also. Maria's husband was another person who showed his encouragement and understanding of the value of higher education. He eventually went back to school and did his degree in Film and Theater. There were friends who let her know that they were proud of her, but her sister's comments and encouragement were the most significant to her. Her mother basically did not believe that Maria was actually enrolled in college. When Maria signed up to begin her teaching degree her mother told her "your time is up for that." She wanted her daughter to stay home and raise her children. But, Maria says, her mother was the one who bought her graduation ring and turned up for the ceremony at the school with tears of pride in her eyes.

Writing poetry was always Maria's favorite activity both during and after the years when she was out of high school. When she talks about those early poems she wrote from the vantage point of age and two college degrees, she says "it is good, but then I realized that even the dialogue was meager." She remembers her dreams of being a writer in high school and the feeling that she would be so glad when she could publish her first book. She sees how the GED helped her on the way to becoming more mature in the way that she made decisions about her life and the role that she played in the life of her siblings. The formal literacy training also facilitated her improved use of grammar. She also developed a deeper appreciation of life as a result of pursuing a professional career, and believes that her poems are now richer and more diverse in subject matter. As a Language Arts teacher, she says, she "learns something new every day," and says "God, thank you that I didn't publish that book with all these errors. God, thank you for helping me further my education where it will have a greater impact." Were it not for the GED journey, Maria explains, she would never have improved her writing or gone on to publish two books while teaching in a public school.

Where it may be true that some people see the GED as a "negative," Maria says that it is a very positive experience in her life. Her understanding of her personal and academic development following the achievement of the GED includes the fact that she is a better parent, because she can share the difficult life experiences with her children and inspire them to avoid her mistakes. "It made me such a big person," reflected Maria, "that I was able to give back." Also, she is a good mentor for her students because "everyone wants to know that they finished high school." If she is able to encourage her students to make good use of their time and finish their studies when they are enrolled in high school, Maria believes, then they can avoid the pain of rushing to make up for lost time as she did after leaving six years' work in the local textile mill.

Maria insists that the GED brought home to her the importance of education and that this is the legacy that she has passed on to her family and students. She makes it clear that:

> When I look back on it, it's not a stigma. I'm not stigmatized by it. [My family] doesn't' look at it as something that was bad. Actually, I look back at it as something that was very positive and would suggest it to people who were in a predicament, today and back then.

Maria is convinced that the GED journey was a "very big vitamin pill" for her. Further, she says, "If I had to cut a pie and show the percentage, I would definitely give the GED 50%, the other 50% good people, and God being the bigger portion of that."

FIVE

# Evelyn Anderson

Evelyn dropped out of school when she was sixteen years old. She decided to get married and raise her daughter, rather than go back to school in the ninth grade. She told her mother, "If they don't send me a registration by September, I'm not going to worry about going back."

The school did not send her registration information for the new school year and Evelyn kept her promise not to return to high school, so that was the end of her formal school career. It was twenty-four years before she decided that she "had nothing to show for" the long life that she had lived as a mother and wife. "Trying to keep a house, trying to raise a child, trying to handle a husband, and learn at sixteen how to be a wife and mother took everything out of her. This feeling led her to ask about classes at Literacy, Inc., where her sister-in-law was attending classes.

The forty-year-old mother also had some ideas about how she wanted to direct the rest of her life. He husband was older and she did not want to be totally dependent on him in case something happened to him. She realized that she could not return to her mother's house as a grown woman; that option was long gone as an alternative refuge if she lost her own home. Evelyn was not going to turn to her daughter in the case of her having to give up her house, either. So she needed a better job and she believed that it was true that "you can't get another job" if you didn't have the GED.

Evelyn claims that she is "lazy" and that it takes someone to "give her a push" before she gets involved in a new situation. She also says that it takes another person to help her make decisions about herself. Because of this orientation to her life, she looked to her GED teacher to give her the motivation to do the practice tests and finally take the battery of tests after two years of studying the GED. She says that she did not apply herself to the preparation of the exam as well as she hoped she would. She told her teacher, Lorraine, that she "wanted to make a good grade," not just pass the test, when she took the GED exam. Her teacher insisted that it did not matter how many points were made as long as she got the necessary score to pass the exam.

At one point in her training at the literacy site, Evelyn sat down with Lorraine and did an assessment of her goals, making a plan of the steps that she would have to put into place in order to achieve her dreams. At the time she did not value the work that she did with her teacher, but, on reflection, she understands that Lorraine was building up her confidence in her ability to make plans and carry them out. Evelyn says that "they also saw that I kept putting [the GED exam] behind me or making excuses to do it later," so they "stayed on my tail until I finally got this GED done." There was also the added incentive to keep working at the GED as a result of being invited to work as part of the staff hired on a grant that the Literacy, Inc. was awarded. She stayed on that job for ten years and is happy to report that her boss was always supportive of her and encouraged her by commending the high quality of her work.

Evelyn found that she did not join in with groups to study at the literacy site. She would use the computer program to do her practice tests in the evenings when she was done with her job. She imagines that this may have been part of the reason that she took two years to complete the GED tests successfully. Although she doesn't consider herself a loner, she was quite content to go at her own pace and do the GED program in her own time. She had a full life with her husband, daughter, and granddaughter, as well as duties at church. Studying and doing homework, especially practicing tests, were not high priorities for her.

Another reason that Evelyn cites for her resistant attitude to the GED journey was her low self-esteem. She says that she would "only talk to people who were on my level or below me." People who "could inspire me or help me" caused her to shy away from their company. It took a determined teacher, Lorraine, and the director of Literacy, Inc., to convince her that she was capable and worthy of the best opportunities that life could offer. "They took an interest in me, what I did, and gave me things to do to show me what I could do. This was my turning point," Evelyn explains.

When she was in high school Evelyn recounts that she always had low grades, and reading was not a favorite subject. As a result, when people at the literacy site began giving her books, she would start them and then lay them aside for months. She put one book, *In Present Danger,* away for eight months before she finally picked it up again and finished it. There were other books that her coworkers passed on to her including *Let me Call You Sweetheart,* and *To Kill the Angels,* and she found herself developing the habit of reading over the course of her tenure at the literacy site.

After leaving the job at the literacy site, Evelyn found herself out of work for about six months. She reluctantly applied to Millers Motel and began a career as a housekeeper. This was not the kind of work that she had envisioned for herself after attaining the GED, but she needed the money. Her longing to contribute to the family budget dominated her decision to join the motel staff. Because of her salary from her work at the motel her family was able to go to Disney World and attend a family funeral in Chicago, and her husband was able to make a business trip out of town. She was also able to enjoy having her own money so that she could help her daughter when she was able to, buy things as her fancy dictated, and take care of almost half of the household bills. These things help her to feel like a working woman who can take care of her family.

When she thinks about her journey to the GED diploma, she is aware that her granddaughter's presence in her life had a lot to do with her continued push for more education. She had this burning desire to be able to talk to all kinds of people. "I want to be able to do things for myself, to be able to teach my child or my grand kids, to be able to help somebody and I can't help anybody until I help myself."

When she began the GED course her granddaughter was in kindergarten; now the little girl has grown to be a teenager and she keeps telling her "Grandmomma, you can do it. If I can help you, Grandmomma, I'll help you." The child hopes to see Evelyn graduate from college.

Evelyn's mother was also very supportive of her decision to return to school; she told her that she needed a high school education to continue to prosper in her life. Her three brothers and sister were also encouraging of her GED studies. Even though these siblings had all completed high school and gone on to college, they never made Evelyn feel that she had made a bad choice by opting for marriage and a family at an early age. However, when Evelyn returned to school and achieved the GED, everyone in her family was expectant that she would continue her studies at Metropolitan College.

At age fifty, Evelyn is disappointed that she did not continue classes at the college level. The demands of work, school, and church did not combine successfully for this student. She made a decision to leave school alone so that she could keep her job and family on track. Fortunately, her work as a housekeeper turned out to be rewarding even though she thinks it does not "sound nice" to say you clean at a motel.

What Evelyn has found out on this job is that she has the ability to "get along with anybody." She knows how to talk to her fellow workers, who call her "head housekeeper," as well as the wide variety of customers at the low-income motel. She also has a very good relationship with her boss, who says that she "never has to worry" when Evelyn is on duty. This makes Evelyn feel very proud because she is considered a competent worker on the job. As she explains:

> I have a lot of extra things to do and the other girls are basically under me or always asking me questions and sometimes the manager . . . is asking questions, so they kind of depend on me. I like that!

She inspires her fellow workers by encouraging them "to value the work." The customers who stay at the motel are treated with respect because Evelyn believes that different people have to be treated with varying degrees of attention in order to keep everyone happy.

When she describes the range of people whom she deals with and the way in which she adjusts herself to situations, she says that "there are old people here and I take the time to check on them because they're just left [behind] and the young people here, I can deal with them."

As far as the benefits of the GED diploma in her life, Evelyn believes that the most important contribution that it has made is in the increase in "self-confidence" that she has experienced since she completed the battery of tests. She admits that she is "big-headed" now and that she believes she can "do anything that I set my mind to." She does not need a GED to be a housekeeper at a motel, but she knows that it gives her the option of getting a different job eventually. Evelyn believes the GED is "like having a key and opening any door that you choose; it all depends on how hard you work for it."

She wants to move on to an office job, and the GED makes it a possibility that would otherwise not exist. When Evelyn talks about her future, she envisions herself joining the motel management in a planning capacity. She knows that management does not take the experiences of the custodians and housekeepers into consideration when they are making plans for Millers Motel.

Her mission would be to inform the company of the issues that the housekeepers face and to make recommendations that would enhance the success of the housekeepers and improve the motel's business.

Because of her success in her present position, she believes that there is as strong possibility of her moving into a higher position at the motel. She also believes that the time is coming when she will pursue further education, though she does not know what field will attract her attention.

Evelyn likes to read the Bible, even though there was a time when reading it was always "scary," but now it talks to her like a "roadmap." One of the things that she has learned from studying the text is that "you have to learn your faith," and that she is certain she will be blessed with the knowledge to make the right decision about her life. She is "waiting patiently" to see which direction her life takes at this point. "Until you are ready for whatever it is God is going to bless you with you just have to wait for it," she says.

Her daughter, who dropped out from high school and then returned to finish, wants to open a day care center for young children. This daughter is now married and has three children of her own. Evelyn is beginning to think that this day care business would possibly be a good direction for her to take her own studies. Owning the business would allow her to be with her daughter and have a chance to use her well-honed people skills. This would be another opportunity for advancement, an alternative to moving to another job at the motel.

When Evelyn talks about herself, she points out her ability "to pull the good out of a bad situation." This is an attitude that has seen her through many difficulties in her life. She finds herself "giving information or giving advice, and sometimes I don't know where it comes from." She enjoys the fact that people call her "crazy" and that she can make people laugh. When she has time off from work, she visits either the older people in her neighborhood or her family. She also does business for her church and is able to get time off from the motel in order to do this work. All of these activities put her in constant contact with people, and she enjoys her success at communicating with them so well. She says, "I'm just an up person I have learned." She believes that her ability to communicate well is a result of the fact that she has "grown up" and learned "to take charge." She's much happier because she knows herself a lot more than she had before her GED journey.

SIX

# Cross-Case Analysis

This chapter begins with an analysis of the responses to the first prompt when we met with each of the four women—that is, How did she come to her GED certificate? We intended to find out as much as possible about her life leading up to her present position or to her status as a GED graduate. Across the four women's stories, there were similar themes that reflected the obstacles that the women overcame before joining a GED class.

The first theme encountered in the analysis was the inner drive to improve each woman's circumstances. Carmen was finally able to return to school after thirty-two years away from formal education. The classes offered at the Women's Center were free, and therefore she did not have the restriction of a lack of funds that had kept her out of the classroom for many of the years that she longed to be a student. She also knew that she had to have a GED if she was going to improve her job prospects. As she explained:

> I found out that Bible teaching wouldn't get you good jobs. You know, faith is good, but you need some education. That's when I realized that I needed my GED so I would be able to get a better job than I went to. 'Cause I always thought about having a bed and breakfast inn . . . so I had to go back to school to get some education, and a better foundation.

Maria returned to school after assessing the prospects of her career advancement at the textile mill. Her observation of one woman who had been on the job for some thirty years helped Maria resolve to do something more with her life. She was also motivated to go back to school after talking with one of her former high school classmates. After all, she reasoned, she was an honor roll student in high school and she knew that she had the ability to do the work even if it was six years after her other friends completed their high school training.

Evelyn found herself wondering whether she had done anything meaningful with her life once she turned forty. She told her sister-in-law that she wanted to go to Literacy, Inc., in order to "freshen up" her skills before taking the GED exam. Behind this plan was the understanding that her husband was older and that he might not always be around to support her financially. She also wanted to set an example for her grandchild, and do more things for herself. This need to be independent pushed her out of her comfortable niche and started her on the two-year journey at the GED program.

C.C., whose children were in fourth and fifth grades, had the feeling that she was not keeping up with their academic advancement. She talked about the need for more literacy training on the job at State University where she was a custodian in order for her to be successful with her work duties. When the literacy classes began on campus, she was among the first students to sign up for the day classes even though she was on the night shift for a long time. C.C. remembers that she was depressed about her lack of reading skills, and the fact that she was not able to understand some of the topics that her children discussed. She wanted to be able to read a newspaper and understand it without feeling ashamed about her low literacy level.

The second theme that runs through the stories of the journey to the GED is the kind of support that each woman encountered along the way. Whether it was Maria, who spent one month preparing for the GED, or Evelyn, who spent two years making up her mind to do the exam, each woman named a list of friends, family, and teachers among the important people in the experience. A short review of the women's comments shows how different people figured in the success stories.

Maria remembered her number one support in this way: "My dad, I think he was the key to me going back to school because there were times when he would always encourage and he would always say to me, 'it is not too late.' So I think that he was a big part of it." Talking about the class of students at the campus site, C.C. remembered that:

> We would all get around a big table and all of us was like on different levels, so we had some people sitting there that didn't know their colors,

that didn't know their numbers, and the good thing about it [was] that the ones of us who knew a little more than them would always try to assist them ... didn't want to leave them behind.

Carmen talked about her husband's role in her pursuit of the GED:

> He told me that was fine to go back to school ... took care of the children, on holidays when I was in school. He picked them up if they were sick ... at one point, I fell and I had to wear a caste ... I could hardly walk but he drove me to school every day cause I had a fit if I didn't go.

The teachers were a special part of each woman's story. Carmen and Maria had particularly close relationships with the women who tutored them before they did the GED tests. Carmen remembered:

> Olivia wasn't only educated, but she had a very understanding heart. She showed so much affection. She loved us into our lesson! She would rebuke us into our lesson, even. That's why I liked her, because she showed a lot of love and concern. But she was also firm. If she saw that you were wasting time, she'd hop on top of that desk and say I want everybody in here to be quiet.

Evelyn reflected about her teacher, Ann:

> It's just Ann does things and you don't know why but you don't really question because you really know deep down within you that she's doing it for you. And it was just funny, it was funny the relationship we had and to me I'm a better person for Ann ... [she] was always there at the door kicking.

C.C. recalled that she "had a great teacher who was always there, who not only wanted to know where you've been or where you're going, but where you're coming from; she was always interested in the whole you. And she helped me a lot."

Children played a very important role in the lives of each woman. Maria had one child when she went to Technical College to prepare for the GED. Carmen had five children when she enlisted at the Women's Center. Evelyn had a grown daughter and one grandchild when she started at Literacy, Inc. C.C. had three children and three grandchildren when First State University began offering literacy classes to the custodial staff on campus. In three of the cases, the women found themselves trying to keep up with the educational advancement of the children in their lives.

C.C. described how she felt in her statement that "when you see your kids growing up finishing school, going to college, it kind of pushes you to want to go further; you understand what you missed and how it could have been for you." Maria wanted to offer a better life to her child and her brothers and sisters, so she completed her GED in order to set an example to the other siblings. Maria recalled that she "was the oldest [at home] . . . and I always felt like a bread winner . . . I did feel an obligation to my siblings in so many ways." She even went on to support her brother's school career by taking a second job "to help send him to college and make sure that he didn't fall away into a textile job, become a member of the credit union, and have a car." She wanted him to realize big dreams, and did the necessary work to see them come true. Carmen remembered very clearly that:

> When I put my children in school, I realized there was things I know and things I don't know. And I truly love school but I just got out of it and to see what they had to do, the things were so new to me, I wanted to go back to school myself.

Evelyn saw her grandchild as one of the main reasons for her ambition to return to school and finish her high school training. As she talked about that transition to school and the GED program, she said:

> I want to be able to do things for myself. I want to be able to teach my child or my grandkids. I want to be able to help somebody and I can't help anybody until I help myself.

Another theme that is common among the women's stories is their ambition for a better life than the one they were living. Carmen, though a member of her church and a holder of several certificates from Bible college, wanted to run her own bed and breakfast business. She saw school as one of the necessary steps to achieving this long-held dream. She also understood that she would have to deal with people in her line of work as a businesswoman, and so she set about getting her writing and speaking skills ready for the time when she had to interact with the public. Carmen recalls:

I thought about the [bed and breakfast business]. I said, "Well, you have to know how to keep books, and things that I would have to do to run a business." I knew that I had to be educated. So I got to thinking about that . . . I said, "I need to go back to school cause I don't even know how to get started and this was the desire of my heart. I want to go and I want to open up the bed and breakfast inn, but then I say I don't even know how." So that's what made me encouraged to go back.

Evelyn heard people say that the GED was a necessary part of the training for securing a job. She took this advice to heart and enrolled at Literacy, Inc. Even though she said that she was "chicken" and delayed getting the tests done in a timely way, she knew that eventually she was going to make up her mind to do the GED exam. She did not know that her first job after gaining the GED was going to be as a housekeeper. That fact made it more important to her that she had the certificate and could change her job when she felt that the time had arrived in her life for a career change. Having the GED was the first step to thinking of herself as a competent person. She remembers how much it meant to her to have the president of Literacy, Inc. praise her in her daily work.

Maria recollects a conversation she had with a woman from her past whom she ran into in the grocery store one day:

> She said, "Well, I graduated from college." And immediately, it felt like a dagger went into my heart . . . the word college, it just rang in my spirit . . . because she was not one of the brighter kids and I was trying to figure out how did she finish school. And so I think that was like a wake-up call for me. If she went to college, even the time that you have been out, you should be able to go back and do something with your life.

C.C. explained her quest for literacy training on the job as follows:

> We would always talk to people that we worked with, like our supervisors and foreman, that this is the university and it should be able to help people that are employees. You should be able to read the chemicals that you use . . . it would prevent accidents from happening because you could read what things are, you don't have to depend on your memory . . . you can pick it up and you can read the label and you know what you're using.

The questions that we asked when we met for the second interview with each woman—"Ask the participant to tell you as much as possible about the details of her GED graduate status, such as

'What is your work?;'What is it like for you to do what you do now that you are a graduate?'"—was followed up with prompts like: "Do you think you could have done what you're doing now without your GED?"; "So what is it like for you in your personal life ... now that you're a GED graduate?"; "How did the GED journey affect your children?"; and "Are you doing different things now than you planned to do when you got the certificate?"

In this second interview, we were concerned with capturing the picture of the GED journey from the perspective of each woman's lived experience. Our intention was to see the GED journey through the eyes of the Black women with children, who made the decision to turn their lives around and face the challenges that being in school represented. We found that the women talked about the way in which their families, children, and friends figured in their lives after the GED was attained.

---

Six themes emerged from the responses to this prompt about life with the GED. The women talked about their change in job status, the impact of the new level of literacy on their children, the reactions of their husbands to the new GED status of their wives, their new level of confidence in themselves, their philosophy of dealing with people on their jobs, and the future goals in education that they were developing.

C.C. talked about the promotion from custodian 1 to superintendent on the campus of First State University. Her description of this new status as a GED graduate went like this:

> I just got another promotion and it makes a difference because there are so many jobs that you can't get that maybe you can do, but you can't get if you don't have a certain paper and that's your GED. Sometimes you be on a job and you can't go any further because you don't have a high school diploma or a GED because that's their requirement and so when I got it, that opened up doors for me that were not open before.

Maria talked about the impact of the decision to do a degree in education:

> Teaching has been great for me. I love it. I don't know if it's because I'm a parent with six children but I understand that to me teaching is

ministry. It's not just a profession. I believe that we have more than a part in the classroom for our children than just giving them information to match. I think we have to be models, role models for all and encouragers, and surrogate parents . . . I enjoy the sport of teaching, I enjoy the art of teaching, and I enjoy the profession and the ministry of teaching. It's been wonderful.

Finally, Evelyn talked about her position at the motel where she was working as a housekeeper:

The GED just gave me the papers that I needed. If I ever decide to leave this job . . . I do have my GED. If I wanted to do some other trade. Right now, like I said, I am happy here, I'm not ready to do any more climbing right now. I intend to be here for a minute. I'm hoping to grow with the company, not always be a housekeeper. So right now my GED is within me, I know I got it, I feel good that I got it.

The impact of the GED on each woman's family is profound. The women talked about how they understood that there were differences in their families after the GED was achieved. Carmen stated:

So I'm still in school in a sense. So when [the children] sit down I'm there with Math, making sure their problems are correct . . . Even in English I have to let them know which contraction to use, whether it's we are or we were, or things of that nature. So I'm right there for them even in the evening to help them through their classes.

Maria talked about the success of her three oldest children:

The three older girls have graduated from high school. One is working on a master's degree in Microbiology, one is a chemical engineer, and one is a sophomore at First State University. And they are doing very well. And then we have three who are still at home. And again, education is the key . . . we are really big on education.

The majority of the women talked about the change in attitude of their husbands once they had achieved their GED certificate. Once C.C. got promoted to superintendent status at First State University, she had to make changes at home. She remembers that, at first, her "husband didn't feel too good" about her promotion. She felt that "maybe he thought I would change the person that I am, but now, he's fine." She also realizes that:

> If I didn't have an understanding husband, it wouldn't be so good because sometimes I have to stay later. And sometimes when you're in charge of something, something comes up, you got to stay there and make sure it's okay before you leave. Sometimes I go home and when I get there, I get a call back.

Maria talked about the fact that her husband "went back to school at forty-seven, to get his degree at Slate University" and graduate with a degree in Family Theater. She commented that out of her "boo-boo came a lot of good stuff," and her daughters and husband are enjoying the benefits of higher education degrees. It was clear that she was very proud of her husband. She appreciated the fact that he had made a decision to enhance his educational skills and be a role model for the six children that they were raising.

Carmen talked about the role that her husband played in her journey to the GED certificate. She pointed out that when she "started school [her] husband had to step in more" to help her. Since he "stood by" her in those nine months of study for the GED, she wanted to give him a break from taking care of the children and the household before she returned to school. She said:

> My husband, he so beautiful, he stuck by me these nine months, he took care of the children, he had food on the table. Now I got to give him a recess, see what I'm saying. He don't want to go through that right now again. And while he's taking a break, I can be spending more time with my children and my household . . . I'm seeing about him for a while cause he hasn't been feeling well.

As far as their philosophies of dealing with people, each woman had an opinion about the way that people should be treated. Based on their experience of being in difficult situations, they had evolved a way of managing people that focused on the positive aspects of the value of hardship.

C.C. would deal with her custodial staff and supervisors based on the way that she remembered wanting to be treated when she was in their situation. She described her attitude in these words:

> It was a scary change [to supervisor] because you been cleaning and now you got to go supervise these people that you been working with and they do not make it easy, you know. So you have to keep a level

head and you have to constantly pray, saying things will be all right and if you treat people right, it works out for you anyway.

She also stated that:

Sometimes you have to write people up, which you know is your job and you have to do it. You may not like it, but sometimes you have to do it and you do what you have to do when you have to do it. But you try to let people know that "I'm here with you and whatever, we're in it together."

Evelyn talked about her work ethic in the following way:

Whatever I do I put my all into it and my thing is anybody that works with me, I want [the workers] to value what they do as much as I value what I do. So my daily job with them is to talk about, instill it in them. And like my boss says, "I don't worry about nothing when Evelyn's around because she's got my back." And I try to be that kind of employee.

In her role as a pastor, Carmen likes to speak to mothers on welfare. She talks about her role in the community as one to "reach out and pull people out." Carmen observed:

There's a lot of people going down in ruts out there in the world, and I been working on them. I been trying to find some candidates, I don't care where they been, they could come from anywhere . . . I was supposed to open a bed and breakfast inn but my heart is in reaching the people out there . . . when I can find people like that, that's where I want to be.

Regardng the increased level of confidence that followed the achievement of the GED, the women were unanimous in their appreciation of this positive aspect of the journey. Carmen talks about her new approach to public speaking in these terms:

It's a very successful life, and I know that if you prepare yourself you can reach people. And by someone reaching me, it has taught me that I can reach somebody else. And to me I feel like a success and to me what I'm doing now is like a drop in the bucket to what I feel like I'm going to do. I'm just waiting for some more doors to open.

C.C. had this to say about her new status as a GED graduate:

You just feel terrific about yourself. You want to do things. You no longer feel that people are looking down on you. But people don't be looking down on you, but it's how you feel inside that makes you feel as though people are looking down on you. And you just have all this self-esteem and you just feel good about yourself and it just makes other people feel good about you, too.

Maria stated:

> I'm still learning . . . life is full of things that you can do better. And I'm open . . . I guess I have an eye for children who remind me of me. In the process, I try to steer them in another way. Not to say that I was a bad child but just to say that you can see yourself in the children. And so you better understand them. As a result of that, you seek to make a serious difference in their lives. So it's all been, in the end, worth the ride.

Finally, the four women talked about their plans for further education. In each case it was a question of the right timing with regard to caring for their families and jobs. To quote C.C.:

> You feel good and it makes you want to go even further once you get [the GED]. And that I haven't found time for yet, but that is what I'm pushing for, some classes to take, because you know that you can learn. I used to feel as though I could not learn. I can't remember. It's a lot of people who have problems remembering things, but it don't mean you can't learn.

Evelyn explained:

> I feel good that I got [the GED], and I find myself lately wanting to take up some kind of class. Maybe not so much a class that I'm graded on, maybe something just to enhance my knowledge of certain things. So I'll probably in the near future look into taking some kind of class. I'm not sure but I do feel like that's probably something I'll end up doing.

In the final interview with the women, we asked about their interpretation of the GED experience from the beginning to the day on which we did the final interview with each of them. Our prompt—"Now that you have talked about how you came to your GED classes, and what it is like for you to be a graduate, what does it mean to you?"—was designed to solicit a reflective response to the experience of returning to school and completing a new level of literacy training. The women talked about their pride in themselves for completing one task that they set out to do. All four mothers talked about the importance of setting a good example for their children; the importance of mentoring people in their community, their interest in going on with their education now that they had a new level of confidence, and the changes that they saw in their husbands' attitudes to life as a result of the new challenges that their wives were taking on.

Carmen talked about the impact of her GED status on her children in this way:

> I say to [my daughter] "you can make it honey, you got all the reasons to make it forward, you got everything working for you, I'm here. That's why I'm not working, so you can't say mama is at work today." And so I encourage them and they have got encouraged by [my GED certificate].

Maria explained:

> I do think that because I completed it, it said this is not a bogus program. It's one that someone can actually accomplish some things as a result of it. So I think it was just encouraging for [my nephews] to go and be a part of it and know that if they worked hard, if they gave of themselves, that they were going to get a diploma.

C.C. talked about her children's reaction to her promotion on the job in these words: "'Mom, I'm proud of you, go for it.' Cause they went to college and they go for it."

The impact of the GED status on their husbands was another theme that kept reoccurring in the interviews. Carmen talked about her plans for a bed and breakfast inn with her husband, and had this to say:

> He doesn't say a whole lot now, he listens to me. I talk to him about my bed and breakfast inn, he says "where's the money?" I say, "well, honey, it's not the money at this point, I'm still getting my children in position," I say, but if that's in my future, I will get it . . . So he hasn't said anything else to me about that because I just went ahead and answered him and told him how it was . . . He's there for me usually when I've got a job to do.

Maria talked about her husband's new understanding of the need to write and be technologically savvy in the theater business:

He understands the need to go back and accommodate the writing, and as a result he went back to school to Slate University to get his degree in Film and Theater. He's applying his talents to my talents and we have started a production company; we feel that it's going to be successful. So I want to be the first GED recipient to have her first production company.

Evelyn commented on her husband's attitude:

He just sits back and watches the seed and just lets me grow. Lets me spread my wings. The last job I had I only worked part time, this job is full time so I do more. I pay more bills, which makes me feel a lot better.

When the women talk about the way in which the GED experience influences their relationships with others, there is a strong thread of mentorship that presents itself in their stories. Maria states clearly that:

What blesses me more than anything is that it has given me tools to help other people become successful. The daughters, I think of the students who have come through my life. I think there are coworkers who have come into my life and many are still a part of my life. I feel that the GED has set the stage for all that. I try to be a forerunner in the fact that I try to bring people along with me . . . It made me such a big person that I was able to give back and I feel like had I not received that, I would probably be a very small person that someone would have to pour into me to help.

Carmen talked about other people in her life in this way:

Now I can tell [people] there are goals out there, there's programs out there that you can get involved in. You don't have to reach the same goals as somebody else, but whatever your goal is, whatever it is that you know that you always wanted to do, what you are better at, there's something out there that you can get involved in to achieve that particular goal.

Evelyn assesses the changes in her attitude to people from a perspective of one who has "grown up." She explained:

I'm a lot more considerate of other people's feelings. So I can learn how to talk with them and not try to hurt them . . . You don't have to be sad or down or hurting others and I just like to be that person that can reach down and remove the sadness and pull the happiness. People tell me "oh, you're so crazy, you're so silly," and that alone makes me feel good because I can make somebody glad.

As far as giving advice to others who may be interested in doing the GED, the women had the opinion that it was up to the individual to find the motivation to do it for themselves. C.C. discussed the issue of pursuing the credential from this perspective:

> The GED, it helps me to let me know that whatever I do in life, I got to put me first. It's more important than anything. I have to make sure I'm happy because if I'm not I can't do anything to make anyone else happy. I got to have self-confidence before I can do anything for my kids or my husband. I got to be okay with me.

Carmen remembers advising women about their need to be focused on the GED long before she completed the program. She told one woman:

> Put yourself in school, give your whole mind to it. Study real hard, don't look at nobody else, if you find somebody is smarter than you are, the only time you look at them is for courage. Or they might actually help you to understand, but don't let them make you think that you cannot make it . . . But set your mind to what you are after and you will get there.

Finally, Maria looks at the GED based on its ability to open doors to other opportunities:

> I think it serves the purpose for a lot of people and that's another reason I can take my hat off to it. It can serve more than just people who have lost track of time, people who need the remediation, and so I applaud it. I was talking to a teacher the other day and she had just left a GED exercise or graduation and she was telling me about a hundred kids graduated. And these were at-risk kids, so for at-risk kids, it's there.

## *Discussion*

A review of the transcripts from these twelve interviews with the four women helped me to see how these women had exhibited the strongest sense of character in their philosophy about life. The support for my choice of definition could be found in quotes like this one:

Evelyn:

College for me was not for me because I guess maybe I didn't want to try hard enough or put more into my job. Because in order to do something it is very important to me whatever I do I put my name on it. And it's either the best or not at all. And I could not work, which I needed to do, and try to stay in school because it was too time consuming.

Carmen:

And like I told my class before I left, I say it's not to the swift or the strong, is the one that endures to the end. I said [completing the GED] took me nine months, it'd take you two years, but don't drop out because when that time is up you'll be right where I'm at.

Maria:

I went back and because of the GED I was able to move forward and live a dream that probably would not have been possible without it. In addition to being a better parent, it had allowed me to become a professional in my field, a mentor for my students. Because a lot of times I think they feel discouraged, but then there are moments you can share with them about your past experiences and certainly the GED is one I would tap into.

C.C.:

Before I did [the GED] I had to worry about money for bills, money for clothes, money for food. And each time you move up, you get a little more money and it really helps out. You know, when you have come from a mother with three and you're on public assistance and then you come up to where you don't need any assistance and then maybe to the point where you maybe can help somebody else along the way, it feels good.

A strong thread of spirituality also runs through these women's narratives as represented in comments about their lives:

Evelyn:

I notice when I read my Bible people are generally older and wiser when he has touched them and given them their insight. So with most of them. I'm waiting for that day . . . I've never been sure but I know one day [what I'm in search of] will come to me.

Carmen:

So I decided it was time to go back to school, cause what I had was good for Bible instructions, leading others to a better life, and teaching them what the Bible said. But that doesn't work in the business world. So I had to go back to school to get some education and a better foundation.

Evelyn:

You teach people in more than one way. It wasn't about a grade point average [with the young student]. It's about showing them that you care and that you believe in them no matter what the circumstances are.

What I also found to be most striking in the voices of the women was their conviction that they could have better lives if they tried the traditional methods of achieving better salaries—that is, completing a high school level of literacy. Their stories gave me an opportunity to understand how the organization of labor could compel people to make choices that took them back to the academic spaces that had forsaken them earlier in their lives.

I came to understand that the need to do "different" or "better" was intimately bound up in the push from traditional institutions to make people do what they felt was against their better interest in the first place (Fine, 1991; Freire and Macedo, 1987; Giroux, 1992). The one compelling reason for completing the GED at a later age rather than finishing high school as a teenage student was the need to make a salary. The hunger to be involved in a more meaningful form of education, more creative exchange with the teachers who people the life of a student, was overshadowed by the necessity to earn a living wage. Not a wage that guaranteed survival, but one that would afford a decent set of circumstances so that body and soul could thrive together. This quest for education was replaced by an acceptance of schooling.

Bright minds turned their attention away from a pursuit of knowledge, in the sense of "reading the world" (Freire and Macedo, 1987), to the soul-numbing challenge of making the daily bread. The work of custodian, housekeeper, child watcher, and teacher filled the daily hours of these women, as it did the time of those Black women who were the first generation out of slavery (Giddings, 1984). The reality of the demands of physical labor compelled these women to take what they could get and make a better way for themselves and their families.

It is surprising to me that I have found myself at the end of this particular road of discovery. How could I have gone on a hunting expedition to record the stories of successful GED students and come back with a documentation of the challenges that our society constructs for those who are creative and enterprising? I am much like Fine (1991) in the fact that she also looked at the experiences of high school dropouts, though in New York, only to hear that they were among the best students in their respective schools before they chose alternative paths. I am left with the reality that the GED represents more than a high school equivalency test. I have to confront the fact that I, too, misjudged these Black women when I began this project. They are not "down and out," as Montana describes some of the people whom she works with in her community. In fact, they are the "up and in," as Montana describes them, that society could benefit from encouraging more than it normally does.

At the start of this book I said that it was difficult for my team to locate and then get these women to agree to do these interviews. Our society doesn't champion the success of GED graduates. In fact, I have witnessed a general disquiet among people who admit that they have friends, spouses, or parents who did their GED at some "late" point in their lives. People seemed to lower their voices and turn slightly away from me as they offered names of contacts that they knew of in the GED ranks. One of my graduate students was momentarily shocked when she asked for the contact information of GED graduates, and one of her colleagues, Maria, at the middle school where she teaches offered her name (Maria) as a volunteer for the project. It is a strange phenomenon, this sense of disquiet that comes over people, when you think of all the people who are enrolled in these classes across the country. The GED is supposed to be a good thing for adults to do, right? Or is it?

I expected these women to represent a group of students who came to a hard place in their lives and took the only course open to them. I didn't expect to come away thinking of them as women who had the potential to be stellar students at their high schools, but who had chosen to walk away from the scene because it was not worth their time. In fact, high school had allowed them to disengage in most cases. I didn't allow these women any agency in their choice. I, who consider myself a womanist in the ranks of Alice Walker (1984), did not imagine that these women chose from among the slim pickings that were offered to them and came away with a decision to shape their lives in the fashion that represented a slight glimmer of self-worth. The actual process of making the decision to join a GED class was tough on their self-esteem. They battled through all kinds of social stigma to come to the place of accepting their status in the ranks of those who must earn their living as best as they could with their limited resources. They completed this turnaround as a consequence of surviving the academic life to which they were exposed in high school.

These women brought their sense of self-determination into full play as soon as they accepted that they had to be the first people to recognize and support their choices. The onus was not on their parents, their siblings, their children, or their employers. Maria, Carmen, Evelyn, and C.C. were the only ones who had a responsibility to their ambition and therefore they had to take whatever measures were necessary to make their lives represent their convictions about their worthiness, even if it meant going through the GED program so that they could prove that they were capable of completing a task as responsible adults.

## *Conclusion*

While it is clear to see how the excerpts from these twelve interviews that constitute this case study help to establish my perspective on this project's meaning, it is important that the reader revisit the statistics associated with the lives of Black women in order to paint the context of this story. At the close of the twentieth century, Black women had not made huge gains economically, educationally, or socially. It is an alarming fact that we are actually slipping from national averages in the area of health care and the ability to take care of our children (Center for Policy Alternatives, 2000).

To say that the GED is inconsequential in the face of the challenges that Black women of lower socioeconomic status face would be irresponsible. But it would be equally scurrilous to say that the GED represents an important benchmark in the lives of women who still must face the insurmountable challenge of racism as it exists in the United States (Tatum, 1997). Structurally, the society has not changed to accommodate the number of Black women who are entering the workforce each year. Therefore, Black women are forced to find nontraditional (in the sense that they still don't believe that it is the path that they were supposed to take in life) forms of employment in order to keep body and soul together. This push to find work, not even meaningful work in most cases, has led to the increase in the arrest and sentencing of young, Black women to prison (Davis, 1983). The conditions under which Black women and their children are living continue to represent a serious national threat to the reputation of the United States as one of the "best places to live" in the free world (Edelman, 1984).

So while we trumpet a loud refrain of praise to the Black women in this study, all of whom are employed and considering further educational study, we must also be aware that these women will be entering academic settings that have not made it easy for them to thrive in the past. The institutional challenges that await them have been clearly delineated in the experiences of Black women in higher education (Gregory, 1999). Unless these women in the project find themselves among a strong support group, a network of like minds and concerns (Dowdy, 2001), they may most likely flounder against the rocks of institutional racism.

Embodied in the stories of these women, still hopeful of achieving a high level of economic stability for themselves and their children, is the legacy of Blacks and education in this country. The will to live, to thrive, as shown in the establishment of schools by free Black women like Nannie Helen Burroughs and Ida B. Wells-Barnett (Giddings, 1984), is testimony to the Black nation's belief in the life of the higher mind. But the challenge of the confounding social environment remains a hurdle that has not been eradicated or lessened since the end of slavery in 1865, when schools for free Blacks began to appear across the country. The obstacles to social advancement for Black people only took on new forms in the twentieth century.

Yet to leave these women and their lives to the test of time, I must make peace with the fact that Black people have come a long way from the days when it was illegal to read or write (McFeely, 1991). Black people are getting hired in places that would not even consider thinking of them as potential workers, and it is true that the number of Black women elected to political positions increased in the decade of the 1990s. We are, I remind myself, moving up the social ladder even though it is at a rate "slower than the eye can see or the mind can conceive."

To understand the impatience that I feel, however, I must look at the nation and then consider the percentage of people who are non-White. I must ask myself what must be expected in the context of a society that has never allowed itself to enjoy the reality of a truly integrated workforce and the benefits that diversity can represent for all? In other words, it is important that I accept the things I cannot change, change the things that I can, and beg for wisdom from a higher power to know the difference. Things change according to the time and the place. What is important to the United States now was not important in 1865, and it will not be important in the year 2100. This line of acceptance is the only path to making sense of my understanding of the importance of education, by any means, to Black women in the twenty-first century.

In fact, a parting glance to Carmen, Maria, Evelyn, and C.C. reminds me of the story of Harriet Tubman and the many trips that she made between the slave lands in the American South, and Ohio, in the North. She kept her eye "only on the wire and crossing to the end" (McCully, 1992). With closing words from the writer Marge Piercy, I pay homage to the resilience and endurance of the many Black women who continue to struggle in the face of the overwhelming odds presented by the matrix of race, class, and gender oppression in this country:

> *A strong woman is a woman who craves love*
> *like oxygen or she turns blue choking.*
> *A strong woman is a woman who loves*
> *strongly and weeps strongly and is strongly*
> *terrified and has strong needs. A strong*
> *woman is strong*
> *in words, in action, in connection, in feeling;*
> *she is not strong as a stone but as a wolf*
> *suckling her young. Strength is not in her, but*
>    *she*
> *enacts it as the wind fills a sail.*

APPENDIX

# Interviews

### Questions for Carmen Montana

*Interview 1*

Q: Could you tell me, Carmen, just for the records, tell me Carmen, who you are where you were born and how you came to be in Hayville?

Q: Could you tell me your life up to this point where you have become a GED graduate?

Q: What's HTI?

Q: Could you fill in some of your life from the time that you walked out to the point where you decided it was time to go to Hayville Technical Institute?

Q: Could we stop for one minute let me make sure my tape recorder is running? What kinds of things did you do, from the, you said you changed your life around, at a certain point, could you tell us some of the things that you were doing when that change took place.

Q: At what point did you decide or realize the GED was what you needed?

Q: Could you go back a little bit and tell me some of the things that happened that led you to HTI?

Q: What was the experience, like taking the test and then going to the Women's Center?

Q: And then what was the next step?

Q: Once you made the decision to take the test and then to go on and enroll, could you talk a little bit about how your life happened from that point.

Q: You said earlier on that the idea to have a bed and breakfast was what attracted you to the GED, because you need these skills to do this business.
Q: Could you tell me about that?
Q: Did you ask questions about running a bed and breakfast?
Q: Could you tell me about that?
Q: Talk to me about your experience in this women's center. Could you?
Q: What other things helped you stay with the course to the end? Besides seeing people from all different backgrounds, all different ages?
Q: What kind of things did they do?
Q: What else did the church do to support you?
Q: Could you tell me some of the things that your husband did that were very, very helpful as you went through your journey to the certificate?
Q: Tell me some more about your teacher, like from the beginning, and then through the journey, and then the end of the journey.
Q: Could you tell me some specific incidents in your journey with her? Things that stick out in your mind.
Q: Did anything else happen at the center to help encourage and sustain you?
Q: Was there anyone else at the center you remember being a big part of your success?
Q: You went to school with a certain idea in your head about school and what you were going to get out of it?
Q: How did that change or how did that keep the same?
Q: You had a certain image of what you would be like when you got your GED certificate. Tell me about that image.
Q: What's the difference between Carmen before the GED certificate and Carmen after the GED certificate?
Q: I know how you came to be a GED graduate. Do you think there is a single outstanding motivation in your life for becoming a GED graduate? Out of all the things that motivate you?
Q: Just one last question cause I know that I promised to be an hour long. How do you know you are a GED graduate?
Q: Thank you very much I really appreciate you spending this time with me and helping me understand your journey. So I'm going to stop for now but I want to ask if it's

better to call and make an appointment with you to meet the next time or if we could do that now before you leave? Which is more convenient for you?

Q: Thank you.
Q: And we had talked the first time we met, about some people you feel I should talk to about your experience going through the program and finishing and what your life has been like as a result of that experience. Do you want to give me some names that I should try and contact?
Q: I think I'm going to turn off. (pick up) You were talking about someone else who inspired you?
Q: Did she talk to you specifically about the benefits of school or anything else?
Q: Thank you.

## Interview 2

Q: Okay, Ms. Montana could you please talk about a typical day in your life before you started your GED program?
Q: What other activities would you do?
Q: Could you tell me about your [church] messages, some of, or one of them?
Q: It sounds like your life was divided between home, family and church. So that was your typical life before you started your GED class?
Q: Now could you tell me a typical day once you began your GED course? And that went on for nine months, right?
Q: Could you walk me through a day from the time you wake up in the morning, to the time you go to bed at night, during this GED training?
Q: Okay, so you get, you get to school about eight-thirty?
Q: So tell me what went on hour to hour between eight-thirty and when you left at about two thirty?
Q: Could you give me an example?
Q: And that would bring you to about, maybe midday? Twelve noon?
Q: And what would lunch be like?
Q: Do you remember any of the programs?
Q: So that's your lunch hour and then from twelve-thirty to two-thirty. . .? Back to the books?

Q: Okay. So two-thirty to about seven o'clock is the kids coming home, dinner, settling to homework, and then what time would they go to bed, usually?
Q: Okay. And then what happens from that time until what hour do you go to bed?
Q: Did you have a favorite subject?
Q: So you slept from about eleven-thirty to about four in the morning?
Q: What were you reading?
Q: Okay so now I know what your day was like, during your GED training.
Q: So you finish your GED training and you been home now a year with your certificate?

*Interview 3*

Q: Okay. Could you tell me what a typical day is like now that you have your GED certificate?
Q: Okay. Um, how do you prepare for your [church] messages? Could you walk me through your regular practice?
Q: So you have your topic and then what happens? You write it down, what do you do?
Q: How do you know when you have a good message?
Q: What services did you talk about?
Q: What's the difference between your day during the GED classes and your day now?
Q: Okay.
Q: What's the difference between your preparation for messages before your GED certificate and after your certificate?
Q: What would you do in the class before you had your schooling?
Q: We were talking about the difference that you have seen in your life between, if you compare before the certificate to after the certificate. How did it affect your children?
Q: Would you be willing to share with me some of your writing that you've done?
Q: Are you doing different things now than you planned to do when you got the certificate?
Q: Anything sticks out like the biggest change?
Q: What are some of the reasons you give?

Q: What other reasons do you give people for going back to school?
Q: The last question. What made you go to Bible college?
Q: Thanks.

## Interview 4

Q: Miss Montana, could you tell us, given what you've talked about, concerning your life before your GED certificate and concerning your life after you received your GED certificate, now how do you consider your whole experience?
Q: The whole journey from beginning to where you are now, how do you think about it?
Q: When you talk to your husband about the experience what do you talk about most?
Q: When you think about the experience, compared to all your other s, how does this experience compare to Bible college?
Q: Do you feel that Bible college prepared you for GED classes?
Q: Do you feel the discipline of going to Bible college over that long period prepared you for the discipline of going to GED classes over those nine months?
Q: When you talk to your teacher about this whole experience, what do you talk about?
Q: I'm thinking, you had some vision about what Carmen Montana would be like when she finished this GED course, something in your imagination, you painted a picture in your imagination. Did you reach that vision, or did you surpass that vision?
Q: When you talk to your closest friend about this experience, what does the conversation sound like?
Q: When you talk to her now, what do you talk about?
Q: Do you talk to her about the other piece of the vision that you see Carmen Montana realizing?
Q: What does the vision look like from here?
Q: What kind of things need to be done, to get to the vision right now?
Q: If you were able to go back to the beginning of this whole experience, that brought you up to this point, and change something, what would you change?
Q: If you went to the center today and you talked to a group

of people preparing for their GED certificate, what would you tell them?
Q: If someone says I'm weak, I need help, what advice do you give that student?
Q: Suppose someone says, well Carmen, you are a strong lady, you went to Bible college, you had all of this preparation to come in here and make the best of this opportunity, you have a vision of where you are going, I don't have that. What do you say to that person?
Q: What do you think your husband says about your achievement?
Q: Okay, I think I have to close up now cause it's time. And I want to thank you again.

### Questions for Carolee Carpenter

*Interview 1*

Q: Can you tell me how you came to have a GED certificate?
Q: Could you give me a detailed description about how you came to decide you wanted to do the GED and then who were the people who led you to the situation where you could actually start saying, "I'm studying for my GED," and held you up while you prepared?
Q: Do you remember any special incident that was really a motivator?
Q: Any special day in the past that stands out in the journey?
Q: Any people who were in the class as you were going through that preparation for your tests?
Q: Anyone in particular who was struggling the way you were struggling and maybe you could see yourself in them?
Q: Did you go back and talk with the group once you got your [GED] since you were the first two?
Q: What were some of the things you were able to tell people to help them?
Q: Anything else you told people to get them thinking the right way to do the exam?
Q: How did that come to you? Over what experience or what incident did that idea make itself clear to you?

Q: Was there a time that your grandchild said something where it hit you, "I got to get this together," or was it several incidents that added up?

Q: Anything else that describes that state that you wanted to get out of?

Q: What gives [you] the idea that [your] kids are better off than you are because you said you look at them and you feel "If I could produce these wonderful children, what can I do for me?" When does the idea or how does the idea come that they are better than you?

Q: So do you know around what grade that started coming home to you?

Q: What was your initial reaction to that fact?

Q: So finally you say I'm going to do something about this and what is that hand that pushes you through the door?

Q: And whom did you talk to?

Q: So you talked to the right person and then you got a way to make this dream come true?

Q: Any other details stand out to you about the journey from your children's fourth and fifth grade years when you say I don't know enough I need to do something and then that door opening when your supervisor says there's help for you?

Q: Did you change a lot once you started this journey?

Q: You think it's the actual going to class or the fact that you made a decision and you stuck to it? What do you think makes the change?

Q: How did your children react when you were on this journey?

Q: If you had to describe this journey in a phrase, what would be your phrase up to the moment you got the GED certificate? From depression to joy, how would you describe it?

Q: Anything else you want to share with me, that I didn't think to ask, that I didn't think to follow up from your descriptions?

## Interview 2

Q: Tell me as much as possible about your work and what it's like for you now that you are a GED graduate?

Q: Tell me about the supervisory position. That was a big change.
Q: What were the duties of the foreman?
Q: So you moved up from foreman to superintendent. Now what does that involve?
Q: What does the GED have to do with any of this that you have described?
Q: Now you talked about your work life, what about your home life? How has it impacted your home life from the day you put that certificate on your supervisor's chair to today? What's the impact of the certificate on your home life?
Q: But how did that happen doing a GED exam?
Q: So, you're saying that the real lesson to learn from the GED is that you should have faith in yourself and believe that you can achieve your goals. That is the real lesson from the GED?
Q: Tell me a little more about the work and how the changes at work affected home as far as you can because your whole lifestyle changed and your sense of responsibility increased with all these people who you were supervising?
Q: Were there special times on your job when this feeling of self-confidence and faith in your ability really changed a situation or brought you through in a whole different way than you could imagine before the GED?
Q: Do you remember a single instance when a situation came up and you said "okay, I'm going to try this," and it came out fine?
Q: When you look back on the GED certificate to superintendent, what things jump out at you?
Q: If you had to give advice to someone studying for the GED what would you tell them is the best benefit of getting that certificate based on your journey?
Q: When you look at the picture of yourself the morning you put your certificate on that chair [of your supervisor], and you look at a picture of yourself today, what's the difference?
Q: Work and home are really different?
Q: When did you sit down and say "I'm going for foreman, then I'm going for supervisor, then I'm going for superintendent?"

Q: So now that you have it, the job, you made a decision to take it. How come?
Q: What do you like about [the job]?
Q: What did your family think about doing it?
Q: What did your children say?
Q: So what do you dislike abut this new position?
Q: Anything you studied in your GED applies to what you're doing in your work today?

## Questions for Maria Walters

*Interview 1*

Q: What led up to your pursuit of the GED?
Q: So what happened between 1975 and 1981?
Q: So in the textile plant, you all were making cloth, fabric?
Q: And what would have been the growth, the hump [on the woman]?
Q: So you said that you had a daughter in the eleventh grade. Tell me about that.
Q: And what month was your daughter born?
Q: So did you go through your junior year up until April?
Q: So you didn't go back after spring break?
Q: So what happened in August when everyone is going back to school and you know you are going to be a senior, at this point, everyone knows that you have a baby anyway, why in August didn't you go back?
Q: So you were a bit too grown for school?
Q: Your daughter was how old and you went back to work at that?
Q: So who was keeping her?
Q: What went on between that six-year span besides working at the textile plant? Was there anything that sticks out other than the hump in the woman's back, and "it's time for education?"
Q: When you talked to the woman at the technical school about pursuing your GED, when did you get started?
Q: Were you working and going to school?
Q: So what about your daughter? Is your grandmother still keeping her?

Q: So, that's everybody [keeping her]? Your sister, your mom?

Q: One other thing, you said that you were working, you bought a car, and did you have your own place?

Q: So you said that you had one older sister, and then how many siblings up under you?

Q: So what impact did your dropping out of school, going to get your GED have on them?

Q: What about your youngest sister?

Q: She's studying for her GED?

Q: So did you have that same feeling as you were working on the GED? What kind of feeling did you have? Did your self-perception change as you were working on it, not before, not after you finished?

Q: So you felt like you were going to college?

Q: How long did it take you to finish your GED once you got started?

Q: Is there anything you want to say about your experience, your life, before the GED?

*Interview 2*

Q: Tell me about your work, what do you do now that you are a GED graduate?

Q: How did that come about?

Q: Who are "we"?

Q: So between graduating with your GED, going to technical school, and then starting college at Witney, you had five more kids?

Q: You began telling me about the fact that you and your oldest daughter went to college together. Tell me about that.

Q: What about work, during this time?

Q: Who was your support system during this time? Who's giving you encouragement?

Q: So that's your class ring?

Q: Tell me about your most memorable experience as a teacher.

Q: To feel like a teacher then, you feel like you have made your mark, you've done what you set out to do.

Q: As our time for the interview is kind of winding up, is there anything else that you would like to say about your life after the GED?

## Interview 3

Q: During our fist two interviews, we talked about what led up to your pursuit of your GED. We also talked about the actual GED itself. Today, I want to talk about what the GED means to you.

Q: What else has happened to you as a result of attaining the GED?

Q: You talked about going back to get your GED, how it gave you self-confidence and built your self-esteem. As a result of the improved self-esteem, what were you able to accomplish?

Q: Well, wasn't the GED just a technicality for you since you were only one semester away from graduating?

Q: So is the GED a stigma for you?

Q: So it wouldn't cause you embarrassment to say, "I'm a GED graduate?"

Q: So you were motivation for your family?

Q: I also happen to know that you write poetry and I also know that you were writing poems prior to the GED as well as after. How has your poetry changed?

Q: I also know that your family is into plays and drama and such. How has education impacted that?

Q: Essentially, what do you think the GED has done for you that you would not have been able to do otherwise?

Q: So are your kids aware of your GED, the fact that you got your GED? Do they understand what it means for Mom?

Q: Tell me how you've helped them with their own educational process.

Q: Tell me about your accomplishments as a teacher, as a writer, as a poet, as a playwright.

Q: I'm trying to get at your GED successes that have come as a result of getting the GED.

Q: If a book was being written about your success and the role that the GED played in it, is there anything else you would like to add?

## Questions for Evelyn Anderson

*Interview 1*

Q: Would you please introduce yourself as to what it is you're doing now and your age?

Q: Would you mind telling me what was happening in your life? What led up to your status as a GED graduate? How did you end up going for your GED?

Q: What caused the low esteem?

Q: Was that at the Literacy, Inc.?

Q: You enjoy [the job]?

Q: You said [you stopped school] because you were pregnant. Right? So that was the main reason?

Q: Why would [the school] not send you a registration?

Q: Do your remember the year?

Q: At what age did you realize [that you can't help anybody until I help myself]?

Q: What was going on in your mind that you needed Literacy, Inc. to keep you on track?

Q: What grade did you end up leaving [school] in?

Q: Now you said you were there for 3–5 years just to study for the GED?

Q: Was the teacher at Literacy, Inc. the one who also sat down with you and tutored you on some of the topics?

Q: How did your family respond when you told them that you wanted to go back to school and get your GED at forty years?

Q: Does your husband have a high school diploma?

Q: How old is your grand daughter?

Q: Did your daughter end up going to, and finishing high school?

Q: Did you have any sisters or brothers?

Q: Did they also finish school, or no?

Q: And how did they respond to your journey to the GED?

Q: So you said you enjoy what you're doing now and is this where you plan on staying for a long time?

Q: So where do you want your GED to take you?

Q: Did you keep up your reading? Did you do any type of academic work at all before going for your GED?

Q: Would you go to Literacy, Inc. for assistance in getting to another level?

Q: Was there something your granddaughter may have said to you, or an event that occurred to specifically make you start thinking [of the GED] in the car that day?

## Interview 2

Q: I want you to tell me as much detail about your current GED graduate status. Where are you now in your life? What is your work?
Q: What is it like for you to do now that you are a GED graduate? In other words do you think you could have done what you're doing now without your GED?
Q: You are a housekeeper; give me in detail what that entails.
Q: So do you believe that having your GED does help you with what you do but you didn't need it to do what you do now? And what I'm also hearing you say is that one-day you're planning on moving on.
Q: What is it you plan on doing eventually?
Q: Is that a position that exists now?
Q: And about how long did you say it would take you to do that?
Q: When would you like to do that?
Q: So what is it like for you in your personal life? You talked about your professional life. What about personally now that you're a GED graduate?

## Interview 3

Q: What did your work on your experience as a GED graduate mean to you? This is totally personal and insightful.
Q: In what way do you have [more responsibility]?
Q: You mentioned the possibility of going back to school. What do you think you'll pick up?
Q: What advice would you give to someone out there who might want to consider going for a GED?
Q: What would that person have to look forward to with a GED?
Q: Is there anything else you want to say about the [GED]?

### Carmen Montana's Friend: Ann

*January 18, 1997*

1: Great. So I'll call you Ann. Okay, Ann, could you please tell me a little bit about yourself?
2: Could you tell me a little bit about what you do?
3: Okay. You've known Miss Montana for a while.
4: Could you give me some of the history of your relationship?
5: Could you tell me how?
6: You knew her before she got her GED certificate.
7: Could you tell me what she's been like since she got that certificate?
8: Could you give me an example of how this confidence shows? Or when you noticed?
9: Before she got her GED, what was she like?
10: What other areas in her life do you see her active in?
11: Have you seen her teach?
12: Could you tell me, describe what a class would look like?
13: Has she talked to you about her experience getting the GED?
14: Did she ever talk about how she got to the decision to go to school?
15: Do you remember any outstanding experience, something that sticks out in your mind about her going through that GED training?
16: How did you feel about her going to school?
17: When she was done, what did she talk about?
18: It's been a year since she got the certificate?
19: Is there any outstanding experience in the year since she got her certificate that you can tell me about?
20: When people talk about her as a speaker, what do they talk about?
21: When you think of maybe the best time you've heard her speak, what is it? Tell me about it?
22: Is there any single time, one topic that you remember her talking about, that you remember?
23: You know her children.
24: Did you see the experience of the GED spill over?
25: Where else in her life do you see the GED spilling over?
26: Her confidence now is different to her confidence before.

## Interviews 81

27: Tell me about where it was before.
28: She talks about her vision. Has she talked to you about her vision?
29: Her bed and breakfast?
30: Can you tell me what she's talked about?
31: What else has she said besides the opening?
32: Any reason why a bed and breakfast? Has she talked about it?
33: Uh, how do you feel her life as a minister influenced her life as a student?
34: Do you think going through Bible college prepared her in any way to stick with her GED classes to the end?
35: Did you think it prepared her?
36: Yeah. The experience.
37: Do you know any of her other relations?
38: Her sisters, her brothers?
39: Did you see her experience affecting them?
40: How does it affect the rest of the people in her life to know that she went back to school at this age and she stuck with it, and she got what she went for, and on top of it she's a minister?
41: Why?
42: Does she represent something special to the women in her congregation?
43: As a mother sometimes we get carried away with how much we have to do for our family, for our children. How do you think her being a minister, and now being intertested in education, affects her role as a mother?
44: If you wanted to wish something for Miss Montana, what would it be?
45: If you had to describe her to a stranger, a complete stranger, and you wanted them to know the most outstanding feature of Miss Montana, what would you choose?
46: Well, uh, how do you think her education has affected her?
47: Is there anything else you'd like to ask me?
48: She talks about you as someone who she sees in her future, because she has a vision of building up a role in the community to help and support other people who are

moving from where she was, from that lack of confdence, not having enough education, into the new place. Has she talked to you about that?
49: Did you feel at any time, that you had lost part of Miss Montana?
50: And what does she represent?
51: And now that you've moved away, how has that affected you?
52: Do you feel that you having your high school certificate inspired her?
53: What else do you think inspired her from being your close friend?
54: You have seen her as a minister, as a Sunday school teacher, as a mother. Have you seen her as a wife?
55: And what is it like?
56: Do you think this GED experience affected that relationship?
57: Uh, people in church have observed the change—have you heard any of their reflections on this change in Miss Montana?
58: When she was going through the training, you were still in the church with her.
59: So what kind of reaction was there?
60: Did people come around looking for advice or looking for a role model?
61: She wants to be a public speaker and she sees this work with mc on this project as part of her, sort of education, about presenting herself to the public. How do you feel about her aim as a public speaker?
62: What would she plan on doing, if she goes forward with it?
63: Do you think she represents something special to the women in her congregation?
64: What would she talk about to the church that the women would listen to very closely?
65: How come?
66: Is there any outstanding memory of something she said that sticks in your mind.
67: Any particular time in your life when she said something that just was right on the money; it was perfect for your need?

Interviews 83

68: When she talked about her teacher from the GED, what kind of things did she talk about?
69: What else did she talk about that this teacher gave to her, that she felt that she should give back?
70: Anyone else at the GED class that she talked about and her relationship with them?
71: Did she ever compare it to her school life before she left high school?
72: What were some of the things they did that made it fun and interesting?
73: Did she ever talk about something that was very difficult to do during the time that she had to put a lot of energy into?
74: When she started the GED program she had an idea about what her life would be like at the end, what she would be able to show the world at the end. Did she ever talk to you about that, her picture?
75: Has she ever talked about how that image compares to the real picture, now that she's done?
76: Uh, she had the idea of what she would be like, and then she became the graduate, she had the certificate. So does she ever some days talk about, you know when I started I thought A B C D, and now it's like X Y Z?
77: When you look at her do you see differences between what she was planning and what it has ended being?
78: Did you have any idea why she wasn't as confident?
79: Do you have any idea where she got this idea that education would make her more prepared, more confident?
80: When you heard that she was going, that she would go for a year, you were shocked?
81: So it was only her health that made you think twice about this idea of going back to school?
82: How did you feel about her actual ability to do the work?
83: So when you heard about her teacher, you felt what?
84: When you see the picture in your mind of Carmen Montana five years from now, tell me what it looks like.
85: When her children talk about her, maybe her oldest, her daughter, what do you imagine they say about this whole experience?

86: What do you think they'll tell their children about their mother?
87: When you think about her husband talking about her, what do you imagine he tells people?
88: What would you like me to tell people about Miss Montana?
89: One more question. When you talk to your children about Miss Montana, what do you focus on?
90: One last question, I just thought of it. When her pastor talks about her, how does he talk about her?
91: And when he talked about her accomplishment as a GED graduate, what did he say?
92: Thank you very much.
93: Thank you. See, you see I don't know what to say. And then you help me. And then you help me, all these things. She's a poet, I didn't know. She's a cook, I didn't know. Not a clue, I've talked to three other people.
94. Not a clue. That's why she said, talk to Ms. J., if you want to know Carmen talk to Ms. J.
95. All these things, I have no idea. I have no idea.
96: Oh my goodness, now I can ask, yes I can ask her.
97: Yes.
98: Does she publish, does she ever share them, does anybody ever get to read?
99: Oh.
100: Yes.
101: My. That is so good to know, it's so good to know.
102: I just thought of something I asked the other person. Do you think there's anything to criticize about her going back to school? If somebody wanted to criticize her and say you know, you've got these children, you've got this ministry, what else do you want?
103: You couldn't imagine?
104: Great, thank you so much, thank you.

**Carmen's Teacher: Olivia**

*December, 1996*

1: Olivia, could you please tell me your history with Carmen, up to today?
2: Could you walk me through those nine months she spent

in that class and then since getting the certificate at the end of 1995, to this year end of 1996?
3: Could you talk about those tests that she had to prepare for and then what was expected from the exam?
4: What exactly are these tests, areas; could you tell the areas? Could you tell the areas?
5: So could you tell us what areas she had to prepare to do the exam for?
6: Could you walk me through a day working with Carmen, what it would look like, from a teacher's point of view?
7: Could you talk about her self-esteem from your teacher's perspective, beginning to now?
8: From the time she got her certificate to this point is a year approximately, what have you observed in Carmen's life post-GED certificate?
9: What kinds of things did she have to work on for her public speaking goal?
10: Has she talked with you about her vision of the future for her life?
11: There were things she learned in class concerning the way to conduct business, since the bed and breakfast was her goal at the beginning of the program could you talk about some of the things that were done to help her realize that goal in class?
12: Can you talk about the field trips?
13: Talk about your philosophy of teaching women in this center.
14: Your student Carmen, or former student, has an image of you. What's your image of her?
15: When she came to you, she had this idea of why she was in that class and what she would get out of it. Did you at any time say, Ha!?
16: Talk about how you came to know that what they needed
would not be in the GED practice book.
17: What was your intuition about how to teach Carmen?
18: Could you give us an example of some things that you managed to work out in practical detail to help her see that?
19: Did you feel there was a point where you knew uh-huh, I've got her, I had her trust?

20: Did she ever talk with you about how she came to the decision to come to school at that point in her life?
21: Talk about how you think your Blackness and her Blackness influenced the relationship.
22: If it did.
23: How much do you think the idea of all women in the group made a big difference to the learning?
24: Was there something unique that Carmen traveled with over these nine months?
25: The classroom you described, and the women in this classroom, make me think that a lot was demanded of you to be able to first intuit what the strength was and then to inspire this person to rise to the challenge that their strength demanded. How did you do it?
26: What have I not asked you that you want to say for the record?
27: Why do you think camaraderie was so important to the women?
28: What was the toughest thing for Carmen?
29: What did you come up with? Things like?
30: In your recollection what is the most outstanding memory of the Carmen Montana story?
31: There's a strong impression from talking to Carmen that you are probably one of the most outstanding reasons that she got her certificate. What's your response to that?
32: Tell me how you feel about these women?
33: Mowing grass.
34: You call them ladies.
35: Okay, tell me about that.
36: Now you, you distinguish that behavior with what? If they were called women.
37: So in your philosophy, being a lady should help them understand if you reflect a positive attitude to yourself, then the world will treat you with a positive attitude? And that is the difference between where you are and where you're going?
38: Do you feel it would have been a waste of time trying to get them to act like women, but different kinds of women? Or was there something really powerful about that lady image?

39: How far were you willing to go into your personal experience of being in that place to help them get the message?
40: Do you feel that a teacher would necessarily have to have gone through those very painful experiences to be able to ground with these women?
41: You feel your experience prepared you more than your actual teacher training for the opportunity with these women?
42: Thank you.

### Carmen's Mentor: Joyce

*January 18, 1997*

1: First thing I need to ask if you agree to the terms that are outlined in the consent letter I sent you?
2: Joyce, could you tell me a little bit about yourself.
3: You've known Carmen for a while, could you tell me about that history?
4. Could you tell me about how you encouraged her and then what you think she should continue to do?
5: ... You knew her before she got her GED certificate.
6: Okay. And she was in class about nine months?
7: Could you tell me about the Carmen before that GED certificate, her life?
8: When she got her GED in December 1995?
9: Yes, so it's a year now that she has it.
10: Tell me what you know about her life in that year.
11: Tell me about her Sunday school teaching.
12: Have you ever observed her teaching?
13: Could you walk me through one of her classes?
14: Have any of the children ever talked about her teaching?
15: You never heard any comments?
16: How does the church react to her getting this GED?
17: When you talked about seeing something in someone that just needed a push to come out, tell me about what that was.
18: When you were encouraging her to let it come, how did your talk buy into your dream of her?.
19: Did she come to you and ask for practical steps to get to be able to do it?

20: Tell me about that experience.
21: Did you feel there was a moment when Carmen believed you, or bought into your dream of her?
22. Tell me about the experience.
23: Did you feel there was anything else in her life or in your relationship that made that moment possible?
24: Tell me about the fellowship time in church.
25: So you were saying that the model of the younger encouraging the older was different.
26: Tell me about how you took on that role.
27: Was there any special moment or moments in your relationship that helped that bonding?
28: Just the six years, and the kind of fellowship that created an atmosphere that allowed you to be of service to her?
29: In her year since the certificate, is there any outstanding moment that jumps out at you that says "Carmen Montana is now a GED graduate," I can tell?
30: Tell me about the moment when it hit you. What was it like?
31: Where was that?
32: At church?
33: In the middle of a service?
34: And what was the church reaction?
35: Describe the whole.
36: What do you feel it meant to the church?
37: Do you think there's something special about Miss Montana that would make the church feel that even more strongly?
38: I asked her if people who would be critical would say you had Bible college, you had that success, you've been preaching, you had that success, you're a mother and a wife, you had that success, then all right it's just one more success. How would you criticize, or do you think someone would criticize this new success?
39: How would you criticize, or do you think someone would criticize this new success?
40: Do you feel that something about the respect she carried as a preacher carried over into her GED experience?
41: You know her children.
42. Did you see a carryover from the GED experience to her children?

*Interviews* 89

43: You're familiar with her husband.
44: Can you guess what the difference might have looked at just based on her, knowing her, how she operates?
45: She wants to be a public speaker. And she takes this opportunity working with me, as a chance to polish her skills and the way she presents herself. How do you feel about that knowing her?
46: Give me an example.
47: If you had to describe Ms. Montana to a complete stranger, and you wanted to choose something really representative, go ahead and talk to me as if I was that stranger. Bring her home to me. If I had to pick her out of a crowd.
48: She took certain inspiration from you. What do you think it was?
49: Why do you tell people they can make it?
50: Is there anything about you being a Black woman that encourages you to say to other Black women go for it?
51: Talk to me about that.
52: Do you feel you're in a tradition?
53: The way you talk about doing it? Making the best?
54: Where do you think you specifically got the tradition from?
55: In Miss Montana, what tradition do you see coming out?
56: Where do you think that tradition of being a good homemaker comes from?
57: If you had to make a wish for Miss Montana, tell me what your wish would be?
58: And what would you see yourself doing to make that wish possible?
59: I want to ask a question and I haven't thought about it before, so I'm going to struggle to make this question.
60: Do you see me fitting in the tradition that we talked about? Could you talk about that?
61: Could you tell me how you feel I can service that responsibility.
62: I want you to ask me a question.
63: I'm trying to create a rounded picture of Miss Montana. Could you give me some suggestions about things I could look into to help fill out my picture?
64: How do you feel her grounding in the church and living

the life informed her decision and then her completion of this journey in the GED role?
65: What else do you think in the church family provided a platform?
66: If you had to tell your children what is the single thing that you should imitate from Miss Montana, what would you choose?
67: Do you remember her ever saying what her biggest regret was once she walked out of school, looking back on her life?
68: Did she talk about how she saw it damaging her life from that point?
68: Anything else that you think I should ask to understand Miss Montana?
69: Thank you.

## *Carmen's Role Model: Ms. Zeely*

*February 8, 1997*

1: Ms. Zeely, could you tell me a little bit about yourself?
2: What grades do you teach?
3: And could you tell me about your church activities since I know you are busy with the church?
4: What kind of activities do you organize?
5: Could you tell me a little history of your relationship with Miss Montana?
6: Could you tell me some of the things that she participated in, in the church?
7: As an evangelist what is her history since you've been aware of her?
8: Have you been at one of her presentations?
9: Do you remember one in particular?
10: Could you tell me about those?
11: Were you aware that she was planning to go back to school?
12: How did that come to your notice?
13: Now she's had a year since she graduated, have you been around her enough to notice her life in that year?
14: Could you talk about what you've seen?

*Interviews* 91

15: How does the confidence show itself? Could you give me an example, when you say that she's more confident?
16: The people in the church know that she's received her diploma?
17: They didn't know it before. Have you heard people comment, talk to her about what it means to them, how it has affected them? Or do they just act differently?
18: In any of her sermons, has she talked about the experience that you know of?
19: You mentioned that there might be people in the church who are in the same predicament; could you tell me how you think of it as a predicament, why?
20: Someone as talented as Miss Montana, someone as successful as she was at that time in her life, how did that predicament affect her, you think?
21: Has she talked to you about her dream of a bed and breakfast?
22. Can you tell me what she talked about?
23: She also has a dream of becoming a public speaker; has she talked with you about that or have you heard that she's thinking of this?
24: How do you imagine that would work out in her life, if she was to pursue that career?
25: Being in your environment, that allowed to hear you talk about your experience as a student and your struggle to get where you are now had an effect on her. What do you think she felt that allowed her to take in your experience that way? What she felt about you that allowed her to take in that experience?
26: Being in the life, being Christians together, understanding the struggle, how much of that is a Black woman's perspective?
27: When I hear you talk like that, it makes me think that you are in a tradition. And I don't know what you hear when I say tradition, but I'm thinking not only Black woman, the struggle in a White society, the struggle for education, but also the tradition of each one teach one, how does that affect you when I say that?
28: What do you think about this tradition that you're in and how it affects Miss Montana?

29: It's kind of too big to answer. When you think about how far she's come in achieving this diploma, what would you wish for her as a next step?
30: Could you tell me why?
31: If you had to describe her to a complete stranger, what would you tell them that would help them pick her out of a crowd?
32: If you had to talk about her to the youth group that you work with as a model, what parts of her character would you talk about?
33: I want you to ask me a question because I feel I'm part of her story now that I've been talking with her for these two months. Could you ask me something that you wonder about?
34: I put this question to Miss Montana. I said to her if someone wanted to be critical of you they might say, well listen you're a preacher, you're successful. You're a mother, you're successful. You're a wife, you're successful. You're a Sunday school teacher, you're successful. Why do you need to go and get one more thing in your basket at this point in your life? How would you react to that kind of criticism of her?
35: And if you were in company with friends where you didn't have to get defensive how would you talk about it?
36: Is there anything you learned from her going through this struggle?
37: Who's "they?"
38: "They push us down, they keep us back," who are you thinking of?
39: Can we talk about Miss Montana as a symbol of hope, resistance, to that force?
40: Like the icing on the cake?
41: Is there anything else that you can tell me that would help me write this story?
42: When you get home you'll call and say you should have said.
43: How do you feel now compared to your first invitation to talk about her?
44: What is it about her that set your mind in that direction, that she already had it? Could you describe?

45: So she managed to develop herself in a way that the rest of us would accept her into the club? You think there's a lesson in that for us?
46: So the knowledge that you saw her using and sharing, talk about that knowledge.

# References

Andrews, W. L. (Ed.). (1986). *Sisters of the spirit.* Bloomington: Indiana University Press.

Baldwin, J. (1995). *What is the value of the GED? A summary of research.* Washington, D.C.: American Council on Education.

Baldwin, J., Kirsch, I., Rock, D., and Yamamoto, K. (1995). *The literacy proficiencies of GED examinees: Results from the GED-NALS comparison study.* A joint study of the GED Testing Service of the American Council on Education and Educational Testing Service. Washington, D.C.: American Council on Education.

Beggs, J. J. (1995). The institutional environment: Implications for race and gender inequality in the U.S. labor market. *American Sociological Review, 60,* 612–633.

Boesel, D. (1998). The street value of the GED diploma. *Phi Delta Kappan, 80*(1), 65–68.

Braxton, J. M. (1993). (Ed.). *The collected poetry of PLD.* Charlottesville: University Press of Virginia.

Brewer, R. M. (1993). Theorizing race, class and gender: The new scholarship of black feminist intellectuals and black women's labor. In S. M. James and A. P. A. Busia (Eds.), *Theorizing black feminisms: The visionary pragmatism of black women* (pp. 13–31). New York: Routledge.

Center for Policy Alternatives. (2000). *Women's Voices 2000.* Washington, D.C.: Center for Policy Alternatives and Lifetime Television.

Cooper, A. J. (1976). *A voice from the South, by a Black woman of the South.* Westport, Conn.: Greenwood Press.

Critzer, J. (1998). Racial and gender income inequality in the American states. *Race & Society, 1*(2), 159–176.

Davis, A. Y. (1983). *Women, race, and class.* New York: Vintage Books.

Delpit, L. (1995). *Other people's children: Cultural conflict in the classroom.* New York: The New Press.

Denny, V. H. (1996). Increasing African-Americans' access to ABE programs: Implications for practitioners and policy makers. *Adult Learning, 7* (3), 5.

Dowdy, J. K. (1999). Doublespeak. *Caribbean Quarterly, 45* (2 & 3), 52–62.
Dowdy, J. K. (2001). Carmen Montana, the General Education Diploma, and her social network. *Journal of Literacy Research, 33* (1), 71–98.
DuBois, W. E. B. (1965). *The souls of black folk.* New York: Avon Books.
Edelman, M. W. (1984). Black children in America. *The state of Black America 1999.* Image Partners Custom Publishing: National Urban League.
Ellison, R. (1952). *Invisible man.* New York: Random House.
Epstein, C. F. (1973). Positive effects of the multiple negative: Explain the success of Black professional women. *American Journal of Sociology, 78*, 912–935.
Farley, R. (1997). Racial trends and differences in the United States 30 years after the civil rights decade. *Social Science Research, 26*, 235–262.
Fine, M. (1991). *Framing dropouts: Notes on the politics of an urban public high school.* Albany: State University of New York Press.
Fingeret, A. (1983). Social network: A new perspective on independence and illiterate adults. *Adult Education Quarterly, 33*(3), 133–146.
Freire, P., and Macedo, D. (1987). *Literacy: Reading the word and the world.* South Hadley, Mass.: Bergin and Garvey Publishers Inc.
"GED Criticized. Correction of erroneously reported average income figures in AP story about people who earn a high school equivalency diploma, high school graduates, and dropouts." 1992, January 21. Associated Press, Chicago, Illinois.
*GED statistical report: Who took the GED?* (2001). General Educational Development Testing Service of the American Council on Education.
Giddings, P. (1984). *When and where I enter: The impact of black women on race and sex in America.* New York: Bantam Books.
Giroux, H. A. (1992). *Border crossings: Cultural workers and the politics of education.* New York: Routledge.
Goetz, J. P., and LeCompte, M. D. (1984). *Ethnography and qualitative design in educational research.* Orlando, Fl.: Academic Press.
Grant, D. S., and Parcel, T. L. (1990). Revising metropolitan racial inequality: The case for a resource approach. *Social Forces, 68*, 1121–1142.
Gregory, S. T. (1999). *Black women in the academy: The secrets to success and achievements.* Lanham, Md.: University Press of America.
Harley, S., and Terborg-Penn, R. (1997). *The Afro-American woman: Struggles and images.* Baltimore, Md.: Black Classic Press.
Igus, T. (1991). *Book of black heroes, volume two: Great women in the struggle.* Orange, N. J.: Just Us Books, Inc.
Krass, P. (1988). *Sojourner Truth: Antislavery activist.* Danbury, Conn.: Grolier.
Larson, C. R. (1992). *An intimation of things distant: The collected fiction of Nella Larsen.* New York: Doubleday.
Lerner, G. (1972). (Ed.). *Black women in White America: A documentary history.* New York: Random House.

Lincoln, Y. S., & Guba, E. G. (1985). *Naturalistic inquiry.* Beverly Hills, Calif.: Sage Publications.

Luttrell, W. (1997). *Schoolsmart and motherwise: Working-class women's identity and schooling.* New York: Routledge.

Maume, D. J. Jr. (1985). Government participation in the local economy and race- and sex-based earnings inequality. *Social Problems, 32,* 285–299.

McCully, E. A. (1992). *Mirette on the high wire.* New York: G. P. Putnam's Sons.

McFeely, W. S. (1991). *Frederick Douglass.* New York: Frederick Norton.

Merkowitz, D., and Wilcox, L. (1996). *Literacy skills closely linked to ability to pass GED tests, new ACE study finds.* Washington, D.C.: American Council on Education.

Merriam, S., and Cafferalla, R. (1999). *Learning in Adulthood* (2nd. ed.). San Francisco, Calif.: Jossey-Bass.

Norris, J. (1992). *Presenting Rosa Guy.* New York: Dell Books.

Peck, J. K. (1993). *The dynamics of ABE social networks.* Paper presented at the 43rd National Reading Conference. Charleston, S.C. ERIC Document Reproduction Service No.

Philipsen, M. (1993). Values-spoken and values-lived: Female african Americans' educational experiences in rural North Carolina. *Journal of Negro Education, 62*(4), 419–426.

Rockhill, K. (1990). Literacy as threat/desire: Longing to be somebody. *TESL TALK,* 20(1), 89–110.

Seidman, I. E. (1991). *Interviewing as qualitative research.* New York: Teachers College Press.

Sloan, V. J., Jason, L. A., and Addlesperger, E. (1996). Social networks among inner-city minority women. *Education, 117*(2), 194-199.

Sterling, D. (1984). *We are your sisters: Black women in the nineteenth century.* New York: W. W. Norton.

Strauss, A., & Corbin, J. (1990). *Basics of qualitative research: Grounded theory procedures and techniques.* Newbury Park, Calif.: SAGE Publications.

Tatum, B. (1997). *Why are all the Black kids sitting together in the cafeteria?: And other conversations about race.* New York: Basic Books.

Taylor, M. W. (1991). *Harriet Tubman: Antislavery activist.* New York: Chelsea House Publishers.

U.S. Federal Glass Ceiling Commission. (1995). *Good for business: Making full use of the nation's human capital.* Washington, D.C.: Glass Ceiling Commission.

Walker, A. (1984). *In search of our mother's gardens.* Orlando, Fl.: Harcourt and Brace.

West, C. (1994). *Race matters.* New York: Vintage Books.

Wilson, W. J. (1980). *The declining significance of race: Blacks and changing American institutions* (2nd ed.). Chicago, Ill.: The University of Chicago Press.

# Index

affirmative action, 5–6
  state support for, 5–6
"Age of, 30 Transition" period, 8
Anderson, Evelyn, 8, 15, 42–47, 66
  attitude, changes in, 59–60
  childhood, 13
  children, 42, 43, 46, 50
  education, 42, 44–45, 46
    high school, 44
  employment, 42, 43, 44, 45–47, 52, 54, 56
    goals, 46
    promotion, 54
  GED
    impact of having, 45–46, 47, 52, 54, 57
    obstacles to obtaining, 42–44
    reasons for pursuing, 43, 49, 51, 52, 64
  granddaughter, 43, 44, 49, 50, 51
  husband, 42, 43, 49, 59
  interviews
    first, 78–79
    questions for, 78–79
    second, 79
  mother, 42, 44
  self-esteem, 43, 45–46
  siblings, 44–45
  spirituality, 46, 62
  study methods, 42, 43
  support network, 44–45, 49, 50
Anderson, Marian, 12

Black women and society, 11–15
Boys and Girls Club of America, 36–37

Burroughs, Nannie Helen, 65

Carpenter, Carolee "C.C.," 8, 15, 13, 27–33, 52, 60, 66
  attitude, 27, 28–29, 31
    at work, 30
    towards GED, 28–29, 31
  children, 27, 28, 30, 31–32, 49, 50–51, 58
  education, 27, 50–51, 53
  employment, 27–28, 49, 55–56
    promotions, 29–30, 33, 53
  GED, 27, 29, 31–32
    impact of having, 29–30, 31, 33, 53, 54–55, 56–57, 58, 60, 61
    reason for pursuing, 28, 30, 31–32, 49, 51, 64
  husband, 30–31, 54–55
  interviews with
    first, 72–73
    questions, 72–75
    second, 73–74
  self-esteem, 27, 28, 49, 56–57
    improvements in, 32
  support network, 28, 29, 32, 49–50
Center for Policy Alternatives (2000), 64
Clarke, Septima, 12
classism, 11, 12, 66
communication skills, 8
Cooper, Anna Julia, 11

DuBois, W.E.B., 14
Dunbar, Paul Laurence, 11

education, 61
    Anderson, Evelyn, 42, 44–45, 46
    Carpenter, Carolee "C.C.," 27, 50–51, 53
    college, 17, 51, 36, 38, 53–54
    high school, 8, 16, 34, 44
    Montana, Carmen, 16, 23, 24
    Walters, Maria, 34, 35, 36, 38, 39, 50, 53–54
Education Testing Service, 5
Ellison, Ralph, 15
employment, 62–63, 65–66
    Anderson, Evelyn, 42, 43, 44, 45–47, 52, 54, 56
    Black women, 6, 11
    Carpenter, Carolee "C.C.," 27–30, 33, 49, 53, 55–56
    minimum wage, 10, 15
    Montana, Carmen, 17–18, 19–20, 21, 26, 56
    Walters, Maria, 34, 36–38, 40, 41, 51, 53–54
    White men, 6
    White women, 7

First State University, 27, 28, 30, 53, 54

gender oppression, 11, 66
GED (The General Educational Diploma)
    Anderson, Evelyn, 42–44
    benefits of, 45–46, 48
    Carpenter, Carolee "C. C.," 27, 29, 31–32
    challenges to participation in, 4–5, 48
    components of, 2
    curriculum, 5, 33
    definition of, 2–4
    graduates
        status of, 14–15, 48
    impact of getting, 1, 8–9, 52–53, 54, 61, 64–65
        Anderson, Evelyn, 45–46, 47, 52, 54, 57
        Carpenter, Carolee "C. C.," 29–30, 31, 33, 53, 54–55, 56–57, 58, 60, 61
        Montana, Carmen, 24–26, 54, 55, 56, 58
        Walters, Maria, 35, 36, 40–41, 54, 55, 57, 58–59
    journey, 7–8, 9, 53
        interpretation of, 10, 57–58
        Montana, Carmen, 55
    passing rate of, 2–3
    perception of, 3, 35, 63
        Montana, Carmen, 60
        Walters, Maria, 35, 39–40, 60
    purpose of, 2
    reasons for pursuing, 3–4, 8, 9, 62, 64
        Anderson, Evelyn, 43, 49, 51, 52, 64
        Carpenter, Carolee "C. C.," 28, 30, 31–32, 49, 51, 64
        Montana, Carmen, 1, 17, 20–23, 25, 51–52, 64
        Walters, Maria, 34, 35–36, 51, 64
    Walters, Maria, 34–41
GED 2000 Statistical Report: Who Took the GED? (2002), 2
glass ceiling, 6

Hamer, Fannie Lou, 12
Hayville Technical Institute, 67
Hill, Grace Livingston, 19

*In Present Danger*, 44
interviews, 7, 8
    first, 9
        Anderson, Evelyn, 78–79
        Carpenter, Carolee "C.C.," 72–73
        Montana, Carmen, 20–21, 22–23, 67–69
        Walters, Maria, 75–76
    protocol, 8–11
    questions, 8–9
        for Anderson, Evelyn, 78–79
        for Ann, 80–84
        for Carpenter, Carolee "C.C.," 72–75

for Joyce, 87–90
for Montana, Carmen, 67–72
for Olivia, 84–87
for Walters, Maria, 75–78
for Ms. Zeely, 90–93
second, 9, 52–55
  Anderson, Evelyn, 79
  Carpenter, Carolee "C.C.," 73–74
  Montana, Carmen, 69–70
  Walters, Maria, 76–77
third
  Montana, Carmen, 70–71
transcripts, review of, 10–11
*(The) Invisible Man*, 15

Kirsh, Irwin S., 5

Larsen, Nella, 14
Lee, Jarena, 14
Lee, Kathy, 3
*Let Me Call You Sweetheart*, 44
Literacy, Inc., 42, 43–44, 49, 50, 52, 78
*Lord, Why Do I Keep Choosing The Wrong Man*, 38

member checks, 10
Metropolitan College, 45
Montana, Carmen, 1, 8, 15, 16–26, 60, 61, 66
  childhood, 13, 16, 55
  children, 20–21, 23, 24, 51, 54
    Maria, 19, 21, 22, 26, 58
  education, 16, 23, 24
    Bible college, 17, 51
    high school, 16
  employment, 21, 26
    as pastor, 17–18, 19–20, 26, 56
  friends, 24–26
    Ann, 16, 18, 21, 25, 80–84
    Joyce, 21, 87–90
    Olivia (GED teacher), 23, 24, 84–87
    Zeely, Miss (role model), 21–22, 25, 90–93
  GED, 55

impact of having, 24–26, 54, 55, 56, 58
perception of, 60
reasons for pursuing, 1, 17, 20–23, 25, 51–52, 64
goals for future, 21–22, 51–52, 56, 58
health problems, 22
husband, 24, 25, 50, 55, 58
interviews with
  final, 71–72
  first, 20–21, 22–23, 67–69
  questions, 67–72
  second, 69–70
  third, 70–71
poetry, 19
political activism, 25–26
self-esteem, 56
siblings, 18–19, 21, 24, 26
spirituality, 16–17, 19–21, 23, 25, 51, 56, 62
support network, 23, 25, 50
*Passing*, 14
Peck, Jacqueline, 4
peer debriefing, 10
personal accountability, 15
personal growth, 15
Piercy, Marge, 66
prison, 65
prolonged engagement, 10

racism, 11, 12, 65–66
  institutional, 65
Rudolf, Wilma, 12

*Seasons*, 37–38
self-esteem, 8, 14, 64
  Anderson, Evelyn, 43, 45–46
  Carpenter, Carolee "C.C.," 27, 28, 49, 56–57
  improvements in, 10, 32
  Montana, Carmen, 56
  Walters, Maria, 12–13, 35, 57
slavery, 14, 63–64, 65, 66
social network changes, 5
socioeconomic status, 5–6, 8
  Black women, 11, 64

*(The) Souls of Black Folk*, 14
spirituality, 61–62
  Anderson, Evelyn, 46, 62
  Montana, Carmen, 16–17, 19–21, 23, 25, 51, 56, 62
  Walters, Maria, 37–38, 41, 61
State University, 38, 39, 49, 50–51, 54, 55, 59
support network, 4, 5
  Anderson, Evelyn, 44–45, 49, 50
  Carpenter, Carolee "C.C.," 28, 29, 32, 49–50
  Montana, Carmen, 23, 25, 50
  Walters, Maria, 35–36, 38–40, 49, 50

Technical College, 35, 36, 50
*To Kill the Angels*, 44
Truth, Sojourner, 12, 14
Tubman, Harriet, 12, 66

unemployment, 6
U.S. Federal Glass Ceiling Commission (995), 6

Walker, Alice, 64
Walters, Maria, 8, 12–13, 15, 34–41, 52, 66
  childhood, 34, 35
  children, 34, 50, 51, 53–54, 55, 57, 59
    Anita, 39
    Michelle, 34, 38–39
    Yvette, 39
  education, 34, 35, 39, 50
    college, 36, 38, 53–54
    high school, 34
  employment, 34, 36, 40, 41, 51
    as a teacher, 36–37, 40, 53–54
    as an author, 37–38, 40, 41, 51
    as a pastor, 54
  father, 49
  GED, 34–41
    impact of having, 35, 36, 40–41, 54, 55, 57, 58–59
    perception of, 35, 39–40, 60
    reason for pursuing, 34, 35–36, 51, 64
  husband, 38, 39–40, 55, 58–59
  interview with
    final, 77–78
    first, 75–76
    questions, 75–78
    second, 76–77
  parents, 34, 35
  philosophy of teaching, 37
  self-esteem, 12–13, 35, 57
  siblings, 35, 36, 51
  spirituality, 37–38, 41, 61
  support network, 35–36, 38–40, 49, 50
  Teacher of the Year award, 37
Wells-Barnett, Ida B., 65
Wheatley, Phyllis, 12
Witney College., 37
Women's Center, 50

## Studies in the Postmodern Theory of Education

*General Editors*
*Joe L. Kincheloe & Shirley R. Steinberg*

Counterpoints publishes the most compelling and imaginative books being written in education today. Grounded on the theoretical advances in criticalism, feminism, and postmodernism in the last two decades of the twentieth century, Counterpoints engages the meaning of these innovations in various forms of educational expression. Committed to the proposition that theoretical literature should be accessible to a variety of audiences, the series insists that its authors avoid esoteric and jargonistic languages that transform educational scholarship into an elite discourse for the initiated. Scholarly work matters only to the degree it affects consciousness and practice at multiple sites. Counterpoints' editorial policy is based on these principles and the ability of scholars to break new ground, to open new conversations, to go where educators have never gone before.

For additional information about this series or for the submission of manuscripts, please contact:
        Joe L. Kincheloe & Shirley R. Steinberg
        c/o Peter Lang Publishing, Inc.
        275 Seventh Avenue, 28th floor
        New York, New York 10001

To order other books in this series, please contact our Customer Service Department:
        (800) 770-LANG (within the U.S.)
        (212) 647-7706 (outside the U.S.)
        (212) 647-7707 FAX

Or browse online by series:
        www.peterlangusa.com